Thirty-Five
Lesson Formats

35

Thirty-Five
Lesson Formats

A Sourcebook of
Instructional Alternatives

Paul Lyons

Frostburg State University

Educational Technology Publications
Englewood Cliffs, New Jersey 07632

Library of Congress Cataloging-in-Publication Data

Lyons, Paul, 1941–
  Thirty-five lesson formats : a sourcebook of instructional
alternatives / Paul Lyons.
     p.   cm.
  Includes bibliographical references (p.   ) and index.
  ISBN 0–87778–244–X
  1. Lesson planning—Handbooks, manuals, etc.   2. Teaching—Aids
and devices—Handbooks, manuals, etc.   3. Group work in education-
-Handbooks, manuals, etc.   4. Education—Experimental methods.
I. Title.
LB1027.4.L96   1992   91–45289
371.3′028—dc20   CIP

Printed in the United States of America

Library of Congress Catalog Card Number:
91–45289.

International Standard Book Number:
0-87778-244-X.

First Printing: January 1992.

Preface

This publication is a sourcebook, an idea-book, a resource for instructors. It contains approaches and techniques for instructors to examine, to tinker with, and to put to use in order to stimulate student or trainee learning and achievement. In other words, these are basic formats for classroom lessons. Some of the formats are relatively new, others have been in use for some time. All are alternatives to the usual "lecture-presentation" format.

Some assumptions underlying this work are:

- More often than not, if an instructor can create learning situations for mature, serious students which permit a measure of autonomy, control, and self-regulation, then there will be greater intrinsic motivation, involvement, and learning.

- There is a great variety of instructional methods and techniques to use with learners, and many of the methods — by virtue of their placement of responsibility for learning on students — stimulate students to more actively engage in learning.

- Most methods and techniques of teaching can be modified and adapted for use in concert with an instructor's domain and outcomes objectives, and with recognition of the partcular needs of the student group.

- Assessment of learning outcomes is not so esoteric that instructors cannot design assessment questions, instruments, and the like to assess and evaluate student achievement.

Many of the classroom instructional formats in this book are based on principles of collaborative and cooperative learning as well as on concepts of group interaction and information processing; and most require substantial student-to-student interaction. The various formats are intended for use with average to above-average students who have a degree of self-directedness, although there are no restrictions for use of any of the formats with students of less than average ability. As creative professionals, most educators and trainers find ways to modify teaching approaches to enhance the learning of their students, no matter what the students present in the way of ability and/or experience.

The fundamental decision criteria used in selecting a classroom format for inclusion are expressed below as questions in the form: Will the format:

(1) place a substantial amount of responsibility for learning on the student?

(2) be potentially useful for application in a broad array of disciplines, that is, somewhat generic in nature?

(3) be relatively independent of elaborate advance preparation, or of software or hardware?

(4) be flexible enough so that an experienced instructor may create domain-specific applications?

(5) present learning goals that are subject to forms of assessment?

Some of the formats can be implemented and completed in a regular class period or two; others may require a few days to several weeks to complete, depending on the complexity of the material selected, the length/complexity of the instructional process, size of class, and the like. Some can be used on a one-shot basis as an experiment, workshop, or lesson; others can be used with varying content, repeatedly (or, iteratively), over an entire term (semester, quarter). Much use, practice, and refinement of these basic formats support the idea that they are effective.

A few of the particularly attractive features of nearly all of the formats covered in this publication are:

- they require no expensive hardware, software, or other materials;

- they place much (nearly all) of the responsibility for learning (e.g., collaborating, preparing, presenting, evaluating) on the students; and

- most require little preparation of materials, in advance, on the part of the instructor.

How can this publication help you?

Here, you have ready access to 35 instructional formats which you can review for use in your classes. It will take a relatively short time to assess the suitability of a given approach. The items are cross-referenced, so the reader may pick and choose items to review which seem to most closely match a perceived need. The items are cross-referenced by these classifications: learning focus, materials, single session, or multi-sessions required for implementation (see Lesson Formats Contents Matrix).

The formats are grouped according to four basic areas: (1) formats to enhance problem-solving and negotiation skills; (2) formats to enhance planning, analysis, and communication skills; (3) formats to enhance cognition and managerial skills; and (4) formats to enhance integration and cooperative learning skills. Within each general category, the formats are presented in alphabetical order for the reader's convenience.

Some guidelines to help instructors use these lesson formats:

1. Don't commit to using a format over an extended period of time unless you have experimented with it at

least once. This will give you the chance to assess impact, appropriateness, management aspects, and time requirements.

2. Normally, it is wise to attempt those formats that really grab your attention on the first reading. You are the best judge of what will most likely work in your circumstances. Your enthusiasm is important.

3. Keep in mind that all of the lesson formats in this publication are suggestions. Most can be enhanced and improved upon by you as you adapt them to your instructional circumstances.

Subject? Discipline? Content?

Obviously the classroom instructor has to make choices regarding which of the lesson formats are to be matched with the content of his or her course and the instructional objectives of that course. The formats in this book are basically content-independent. Most can be used successfully in instruction in areas ranging from the social sciences to the humanities to professional subject matter. Many can be used successfully in the natural sciences. The ideas have been used in middle schools and high schools, colleges/universities, corporate training and management development, and in adult and continuing education.

Table of Contents

ix

The Lesson Formats
(in Alphabetical Order)

Thirty-Five
Lesson Formats

Part One

Formats to Enhance Problem-Solving and Negotiation Skills

1

The Boss Is Away*

PURPOSE

The purposes of this approach are to have students: apply principles and concepts in an applications activity; engage in a team project that creates some cognitive and emotional realism; and demonstrate problem-solving skills in an ambiguous task. This approach has great flexibility and can be adapted to many (fictional) practice-based settings, such as a small or large business, a department of a business, school, hospital, etc. The instructor shapes the details and the focus of the approach to meet his/her instructional objectives.

SIZE OF GROUP

Twelve or more students are required for this approach.

MATERIALS NEEDED

Three items (minimum, but there could be more) of information are necessary for this approach. All items should be prepared prior to the commencement of the activity. The first item is the set of instructions given to the students to get them started on their task. Here is an *example*:

The boss has decided that some areas need careful development in the business and has asked you to develop plans for achieving success in these areas. Here are the areas:

*Adapted from Hale, John F. 1986. The boss is away. *Organizational Behavior Teaching Review*, 10 (3): 107-111.

1. The creation of a human resources department that will serve the needs of the business and its employees.

2. The identification and specification of a strategic planning process to help guide the business.

3. The development of a viable, results-oriented affirmative-action program.

Your job is to do the following:

a. Prepare a list of objectives for each area.

b. Propose the organization design, coordination, charter, etc., needed to achieve success in each area.

c. Specify the human resources, controls, incentives, etc., needed in order to achieve success in each area.

The remaining two (or more, depending) items take the form of letters, telegrams, etc., which the instructor imposes on the students as they are in the midst of making progress with their tasks. The information in the correspondence is from the instructor as agent of the boss, Iam N. Charge.

Here is an example:

To: Staff
From: Iam N. Charge

Have just learned from parent corporation headquarters that major goal is to increase proportion of minority managers by 80% over the next three quarters. We must comply. More interesting news: market share for our soap, FROGGY, has dropped 38% in the last quarter and absenteeism in the FROGGY plant has increased by 40%. Your plans need to be responsive to these matters.

TIME REQUIRED

About four hours are required to process the whole activity. More time is required if the instructor adds several embellishments.

ADVANCE PREPARATION

None, but see "Materials" above.

PROCESS

1. The student group will need to be divided into teams of from 4 to 6 each, with a mix of characteristics (age, gender, level of experience, etc.).

2. The instructor should tell the students that the activity is to test their decision-making skills in an ambiguous task situation. The instructor is to be an observer only, not a resource person. The whole activity is to take about four hours (it may take place over one, two, or more class periods).

3. The basic instructions are given to all students; and, after any questions are answered, the students are on their own.

4. At about the mid-point of the second hour, the instructor gives the students correspondence #1 (see example above).

5. At about the mid-point of the third hour, the instructor gives the students correspondence #2. This second memo or letter is intended to throw a bit of a "monkey-wrench" into the work of the students. The instructor should prepare a suitable memo or letter, intended to create "problems" for the students.

6. Reports. The teams report the results of their work. This activity should be limited to about 20 minutes per team.

7. Summary. The instructor leads this activity. Included should be a discussion regarding:

a. The application of theory and concepts.

b. Reactions/responses to the turbulence created by the correspondence.

c. What was learned about one's skills, attitudes, etc., and about group functioning.

d. The quality of the results.

2

Brainstorming the Agenda

PURPOSE

The purposes of this approach are to have the students: consider their needs and preferences with regard to the course, express learning outcomes that are attractive to them, and to set some tentative bounds/limits on the content of the course.

SIZE OF GROUP

Eight or more persons are needed for this approach.

MATERIALS NEEDED

Chalkboards will do, but large sheets of paper (2' × 3'), felt-tipped markers, masking tape are preferred.

TIME REQUIRED

Approximately one hour is needed for this approach.

ADVANCE PREPARATION

None.

PROCESS

Introduction: This format is most often used as a type of "ice-breaker" activity. The potential benefits of the approach go far beyond personal introductions, small-group interaction, and tension release. The approach can yield much information about the students (their knowledge, interests, preferences, level of articulateness, quality of expression, level of intensity, willingness to take risks, and so on).

This activity can take place at the first session of a course with the entire course as the topic under consideration, or it can be conducted at the beginning/commencement of an important part of a course. For example, in a basic course on Real Estate, this approach may be used when you get to the topic of Listings; or, in a course in Human Resource Management, the approach may be used for the topic, Managing Grievances.

1. Ask the students to list for a small group activity what things (topics, etc.) they want to see discussed, presented, etc., with regard to the course (or topic). (10 minutes)

2. Place the students in small groups of 3 to 5 members. From their individual lists and anything else that emerges from their interaction, put together a list of everything they can think of. There are no "bad" or "wrong" entries, and the small groups are not to evaluate information given, just list it. All group responses should be printed on the board or the large sheets of paper. The ideas and suggestions should be discussed within the group so that the members would have clarification opportunities. (20-25 minutes)

3. The ideas/suggestions sheets are taped to walls around the room so all can see them. Each small group will have a representative who briefly explains what is on his/her respective list. Clarifications should be sought at this time—but—no evaluation of the quality, etc., of the idea or suggestion. (20 minutes or more, depending on the number of groups)

4. When all groups have had their lists presented, duplicate list items are stricken, and all items are still on the walls for all to view. The students are asked to carefully study all the items and decide which four items are most important to them. (5 minutes)

5. Then, the instructor gives each student four colored sticker-dots (blue, red, green, white) with blue as number one choice, red as number two, and so on, and asks them all to go and place the dots on the items of their choice. (10 minutes)

6. The instructor collects the sheets and calculates the agenda from the colored dots-data completed by the students. The information resulting from this calculation can be reported at a later class meeting.

Obviously, the instructor has great latitude in the integration of these ideas/suggestions in the course.

List of Events

1. Participants are asked to generate lists of (possible) topics.

2. Small groups are formed.

3. Groups discuss, compose topics lists.

4. Lists are posted on walls.

5. List entries are explained/clarified, but not evaluated.

6. Duplicate topics are stricken (may require some negotiation).

7. Individually, participants vote for topics.

8. Instructor tabulates votes; reports results to participants.

3

Four "ACES" Decision-Making Method*

This approach is highly specific yet simple. It is intended, fundamentally, to have people get "un-stuck" on a decision and to overcome procrastination via greater focus and vigilance. Its educational value lies in the approach's ability to evoke: varied responses; reflection on personal decision-making styles; and a determined focus on taking action. Basically, the approach helps one to challenge assumptions, the value/weight given to decision criteria, and the set of alternatives under consideration. "ACES" stands for Assumptions, Criteria, Evoked Set, and Start.

PURPOSE

The purposes of this approach are to have students overcome various traps of decision-making, such as accepting an initial course of action without giving it sufficient thought; changing to a different course(s) of action; and being unable to decide among alternative choices. Students may apply the tools of the approach to both academic and personal matters.

SIZE OF GROUP

Any size of group will do.

*Adapted from Pate, L. 1987. Improving managerial decision making. *Journal of Managerial Psychology*, 2(2): 9-15.

MATERIALS NEEDED

The only materials students need are 4 to 6 pages of blank paper.

TIME REQUIRED

Approximately 75 minutes are required for this approach.

ADVANCE PREPARATION

None.

PROCESS

Introduction: The instructor introduces the topic and explains how the problem-solving or decision-making tool to be used will assist one to take action on matters in a timely, well-reasoned way.

Part 1: The student labels four sheets of paper, at the top, A, C, E, and S, respectively. On the top of the "S" sheet the student writes the problem, issue, etc., to be addressed. A personal problem or issue may be a good way to try out the approach; for example, whether to buy a certain brand of car, or to adopt a cat.

Part 2: On the A, C, E pages, the student draws a line down the center of the page, top to bottom. Then, on these three pages as labelled, A, C, E, the student lists, in some detail, the assumptions ("truths," beliefs, etc.), the criteria (rules to govern choices), and the evoked set of alternative entries, on the left side of the sheets, respectively. This will take some time and will be a first pass on the information that comes immediately to mind.

Part 3: On the right side of the pages, A, C, E, respectively, the student now writes down an alternative view of the problem. This is done by writing down a list of counter-assumptions (A); writing a list of counter-weights/values for criteria (C); and expanding the evoked set of alternatives (E).

Part 4: The activities in Part 3 could be repeated with more information, etc., added to the counters and expansion, but this reiteration may not be necessary. From the increased focus and vigilance offered via Parts 1-3, the student should now be prepared to list on page S the specific action steps to take in resolving the problem.

PAGE LAYOUT FOR FOUR ACES

4

Policy–Procedures Analysis

This technique isolates two basic types of activity in organizations; the development of policy and its implementation. Often, the two are not integrated as well as they might be, since different people are responsible for the various tasks. The technique is especially useful in instruction in courses in areas such as: public health, business management, education, and public administration. It can precede an important course topic or could serve to conclude an essential topic.

PURPOSE

The purposes of the activity are to assess communication and analysis skills, enhance ability to formulate and explain a course of action, and further ability to select and use methods and techniques appropriate for the topic under discussion.

SIZE OF GROUP

Up to 80 students.

MATERIALS NEEDED

None.

TIME REQUIRED

Approximately three hours are needed.

ADVANCE PREPARATION

None.

PROCESS

1. An important issue for the course must be identified. For example, for a course in Human Resources Management, one could use a topic such as: Responsibility of managers/ supervisors to conduct effective performance appraisal interviews with employees. This is a fairly complex example.

2. Approximately one-half of the students are given the assignment to prepare a company (organization) policy statement on the topic identified. The statement should be no more than a page in length, and a list of assumptions may be submitted with the statement. The remaining half of the students are to prepare a plan of activities, events, intended outcomes, etc., which would assist the organization to insure that the responsibility identified (above) would be effectively carried out. What would be done and why it would be done would comprise the written assignment for these students. The instructor and the class members need to reach agreement on criteria for quality of policy statements and implementation plans. Once established, these criteria can be put in list form and given to students. They become the grading criteria for the instructor.

3. The work is to be handed-in by students. The instructor should grade the materials according to criteria previously revealed to the students.

4. Students meet during class time, in respective groups (policy or implementation), and prepare a consensus statement of their positions on the matter in question.

5. Then, each group briefs the other on its position, with all class members recording notes on how the policy and implementation procedures may conflict or reinforce one another.

6. Following this, a whole-class discussion takes place in which a sound policy statement is developed and an articulated, effective implementation procedure is matched to it.

5

Practitioner's Desk/In-Basket

PURPOSE

The purpose of this approach is to create a situation where the student has to establish criteria, priorities, and strategy based on time-sensitive information inputs.

This approach is nearly always practice-based. We focus on an individual engaged in some practice (nurse, manager, clergyman, etc.) or a group (committee) that is faced with several inputs of information (mail, phone calls, messages, visitor-at-the-door). Under time constraints, he or she has to develop an action plan premised on some criteria. The approach has enjoyed extensive use in management development and training activities and in corporation management-assessment centers.

The possibilities are boundless, for example:

- a person campaigning for public office;
- a housewife/homemaker with small children;
- a real estate salesperson;
- chairperson of a budget committee of a church;
- a supervisor of a hospital cafeteria; or
- a fourth-grade teacher.

For any one role, a set of items of information, on paper, can be prepared. Then, the items are to be considered, in total, and a plan of action with justification is prepared. Individuals or small groups can take on the role.

Obviously, the bulk of the learning for the group will occur as the choices, strategies, rationales, etc., are explained, clarified, and discussed in a whole-class setting. The approach is driven by two important considerations: (1) what the activity is supposed to achieve; and (2) is this approach a substantive way in which to achieve the objectives?

SIZE OF GROUP

Eight or more persons are required for the activity.

MATERIALS NEEDED

The seven to ten information items, such as memos, messages, visitor-drop-ins, etc., are to be prepared prior to the session in which they are to be applied. The instructor or a class committee could do this.

TIME REQUIRED

At least one hour is required for the activity.

ADVANCE PREPARATION

None.

PROCESS

1. Announce the setting, situation, etc. (3-5 minutes)

2. Select, choose, volunteer the role players. (5 minutes)

3. Provide the information items. Read each one aloud to the entire group (class) and hand them to the role players. (8 minutes)

4. Reality-check on what is supposed to happen. That is, ask the role player(s) to say out loud what they are to do. (2 minutes)

5. Individuals or groups decide how to manage the tasks, etc., that the information suggests. (20 minutes)

6. Reporting and discussion. This will take from 25 to 35 minutes, depending on the complexity of the information, debate, and discussion regarding the judgments made, etc.

7. Evaluation. Some serious attention should be directed to the efficacy of the approach, the materials, etc. It is important to solicit student feedback on these things so that the approach and its attendant elements can be improved for future use.

Role/Situation Example: Practitioner's In-Basket

Role: You are the office manager of a regional claims department for a major health insurance company.

Situation: You are in your sunny, corner office quietly preparing for an important meeting with your boss. These things (below) happen within a short period of time. What should you do? What criteria guide your decisions?

Interruptions:

1. Your teen-aged son has arrived and tells you that the car won't start.

2. A facsimile has just been received from an attorney who claims to represent one of your clients.

3. Your phone begins to ring. You were expecting a call from your boss.

4. Your secretary pops in to tell you two things:
   a. a representative of an important vendor has shown up, unannounced; and,
   b. three of the new (computer) super workstations have malfunctioned and cannot access the information system.

5. . . . . and so forth.

6

Problem-Driven Learning

PURPOSE

The purposes of this approach are to have students: consider and reflect upon a variety of problems that can take place in the context of the topics/subjects/disciplines under consideration in the course; practice research and questioning skills; and work with "real" problems and issues.

SIZE OF GROUP

There are no restrictions on size of group.

MATERIALS NEEDED

None.

TIME REQUIRED

Depending on the complexity, detail, etc., of the problems identified, the time needed for the activity can range from one hour to several hours.

ADVANCE PREPARATION

Within the context of the course, instructor objectives, and so on, the instructor will need to have identified several (6-10) problems that are real and that students can understand. The sources for these problems can be: practitioners, textbooks, research publications, popular literature, and the like. An example of a problem in a course in Human Resource Management: many employers are faced with hiring an increasingly under-educated population of recent high school graduates; or, a course in real estate: full-service financial institutions may render the small, local real estate firm obsolete.

PROCESS

1. List the problems for students so all can see (chalk-board or handout).

2. Discuss each problem as to what the words mean (broad interpretations—few limitations). Some students may contribute suggestions so as to modify the way the problem is stated. This is satisfactory, within reason. The instructor, after all, does not "own" the problem.

3. The whole class or small groups of students can discuss the problems to identify the importance (priority) of the various problems.

4. Problem investigation. This is basically a homework assignment. Individually, or in small teams (2-4 members), the students are to bring to a future class meeting prepared responses to questions such as these:

   a. how do we know the problem(s) exist?
   b. what are some of the causes of the problems?
   c. what are some alternative ways of dealing with the problems?
   d. what alternatives may have the greatest potential payoff: according to what criteria?

5. At the future class session, the body of responses provides a rich set of information regarding sources; research methods used; limitations of the information; the effects, intended and unintended, of the various alternatives, and so on. At this or subsequent sessions, lecture/discussion can be keyed to what was determined by the class relative to the problem(s); additional assignment/research can spring from this activity; finally, the agenda for the course could spring from this activity.

7

Reflective Controversy*

PURPOSE

The purposes of this approach are to have students learn to: study/research an issue; collaboratively prepare a justifiable position on an issue; engage in a consensual process where synthesis and integration of ideas can be achieved.

SIZE OF GROUP

To use this approach a minimum of 12 students is desirable. These should be multiples of four students.

MATERIALS NEEDED

None.

TIME REQUIRED

This approach will require several hours in most instances. Some of the required work will need to occur during class time, while other student work will take place, of necessity, outside class.

*Adapted from Kurfiss, J. 1987. The reasoning-centered classroom: Approaches that work. *American Association for Higher Education Bulletin*, March/April: 12-14.

ADVANCE PREPARATION

The instructor will need to identify some controversial issues pursuant to the subject matter of the course. The issues
may be more or less volatile; however, they each should have
some researchable basis. That is, students will need some access to material (books, journals, magazines, newspapers, etc.)
to assist them in their efforts.

PROCESS

1. The instructor introduces several issues of controversy
regarding the subject matter of the class/course. It also may be
desirable to elicit additional issues of controversy from the class
members.

2. The instructor places students into groups of four. The
groups are to be heterogeneous according to appropriate criteria (gender, age, race, experience, ability, etc.). This is important. A variant on this placement would be to allow students to
form their own four-person groups, or to allow students to
choose a controversy (issue) on which to work. Experience has
shown that on first attempts at the approach, instructor-made
placements are most effective.

3. In each group, two students (sub-groups) study material favoring one viewpoint of the controversy (e.g., capital
gains tax, out-of-state garbage in landfills, collective bargaining
for public employees, etc.) while the other two students study
material favoring an opposing viewpoint. Obviously, some issues have several facets. Time will be required for planning,
organization, and research.

4. Each sub-group presents its findings (oral, written,
etc.) to the other sub-group. No attempt is made at oral persua-
sion; this is merely an exchange of information.

5. The sub-groups switch roles; they now are to study
material favoring the view they previously opposed and are to
prepare a synthesis of their own.

6. Once the sub-groups have completed the assignment
for step 5, all four members work together to reach consensus

on the controversy and to prepare a report representing the group's views.

7. Additionally, any student of any group may write/prepare a report for any (individual) position.

Some Suggestions:

a. If the work is to be graded, it is desirable (as part of step 2) to collaborate with the students on grade elements and criteria. At the very least, the instructor can outline the basic expectations he/she has for student performance in the various steps of the activity.

b. For a culmination of step 6, groups may make presentations to the class regarding the synthesis of the group findings.

Part Two

Formats to Enhance Planning, Analysis, and Communication Skills

8

Action Roles–Structured

PURPOSE

The purposes of this approach (and see also Action Roles–Unstructured) are to give students opportunities to: internalize a situation and act out behavior vis-a-vis concepts, theories, etc., under current consideration in the course; practice communication and interpersonal skills; and to experiment with behavior they may not ordinarily choose to use.

Action Roles allow students to experiment in a safe environment with behavior and information that may be quite threatening to use in real-life situations. While Action Roles are not very effective for presenting/communicating information, they are useful for practicing interpersonal and communication skills and for the demonstration and elaboration of abstract ideas and concepts. Situations (roles) and attendant skills can range from relatively simple matters, such as welcoming people to a reception for a state politician, to very complex and emotionally-charged matters, such as the termination of employment of an individual.

Action Roles are a highly generative activity for role-takers and participants-as-observers because the approach encourages a variety of alternative responses and initiatives; and, affective, cognitive, and prescriptive elements of behavior are present, together, in most applications. It is a rich tapestry.

The instructor needs to have a sense of confidence in the management of an approach such as this because a safe, trusting, accepting environment is required for students to operate freely. The instructor needs to be viewed as one who is encouraging, non-coercive, and open.

Some features of the approach are:

1. It provides opportunity for practice of both communication and interpersonal skills.

2. Much information for definition, analysis, and evaluation is generated.

3. It presents an experience which the students have in common and can use as a point of reference.

4. It encourages active participation.

5. The approach can easily be used to focus on the specific application of theories, concepts, skills, etc., under consideration by the class.

6. Finally, the approach may be helpful in encouraging attitude change because evaluation will identify, in the company of knowledgeable peers, behaviors deemed appropriate or inappropriate.

It is most important that this approach as an activity be taken seriously by the students. While it can be fun, novel, and invigorating for most students, it is not play (never call it role *play*), and special effort needs to be made by the instructor so that the activity does not result in simplistic responses.

SIZE OF GROUP

At least ten persons are needed in the approach.

MATERIALS NEEDED

Suppose you design an activity (a situation) with three roles. Each role requires a description which may include the role's attitudes, beliefs, knowledge of the situation (problems, issues, etc.) and knowledge of other actors (roles), and so on. Obviously, the roles are substantially different and focused on the instructional purpose you have in mind. Each role description should require no more than one typed page of material, double-spaced. More than four or five roles in the activity can become a very difficult matter to manage. Quantities of materials depend on the choice of involvement you make (see Process, below).

TIME REQUIRED

It is very difficult to estimate time needed to carry out Action Roles. Obviously, time requirements are tied to the complexity, comprehensiveness, etc., of the material in question and the discussion that attends the role performance. At least one hour is normally required for the complete process.

ADVANCE PREPARATION

(see above)

PROCESS

1. The role-takers are identified and provided with the structured role materials and instructions. (10 minutes)

2. The role-takers can be a single group of individuals that act out the roles before the rest of the class (observers); or, sets of role-takers can be identified, each with a small number of observers. In essence, the entire class can be more directly involved in the second instance. Both forms have strengths and limitations.

3. The instructor takes the time to provide structure to all with regard to what the situation is about and its relationship to what is being studied. (10 minutes)

4. The action roles are performed. It is desirable for the task, issue, problem, etc., to achieve a conclusion. (30 minutes)

5. Feedback and assessment. This phase is very important, as role-takers have the opportunity to discuss feelings and emotions taken/released during the performance; discussion as to the effectiveness of certain behaviors relative to learning ob-

jectives takes place; and all class members have an opportunity from either point-of-view: role-taker or observer. (20-30 minutes)

Examples

Here are roles/descriptions of the three members of the Paradise County Board of Education. The Board is preparing to vote on the annual budget of the county schools.

IRMA FRIENDLY

I'm glad I didn't campaign on the no-new-taxes theme because our schools need help and we've got to obtain the money to help the education professionals do their jobs. Our needs are many. Our teachers are the lowest paid in the state, and low morale and low self-esteem are carrying over to the classroom. We need new instructional resources, equipment, and supplies. We are going to lose good teachers to neighboring counties if we cannot improve working conditions and support the educators.

EDGAR TUFF

From what I can tell, the schools in this county, particularly the high schools, are out of control. Things have been sliding downhill for years. We have fewer kids going on to college, drug use is a major problem in the schools, truancy and absenteeism are out of sight. The educators want more money. Just give us more money, they say. Well, we have to hold them accountable for turning some of these problems around. When I see some positive effort and results, then I'll be willing to consider new taxes and more money for schools.

SALLY NOOTRAL

I'm new on this board and I've got a lot to learn. To have to make important decisions about finances and the budget is a huge task, and there is a lot of information I need in order to make informed decisions. Unfortunately, I've had little time to do my homework. I haven't formed any major opinions about the significant issues, yet. I have an open mind on the whole thing, I believe, and I need to do much more study of issues and finances.

9

Action Roles–Unstructured

Basically, this approach is the same as Action Roles–Structured, hence the material explaining that approach should be consulted. The differences are as follows:

1. Role-taking (assignment) takes place on-the-spot, spontaneously, with no special information provided in writing to any of the role-takers.

2. While the instructor needs to know how and when to move to the Action Roles, the instructor does not have to prepare materials solely for the role-taking task.

3. Usually, a higher level of trust, comfort, etc., needs to exist in the class to use this approach (as compared to the Structured approach).

4. The time required for the Unstructured approach to be completely processed may be less predictable than that for the Structured approach.

10

Committee Decision

PURPOSE

The purposes of this activity are to have students: seriously consider reading assignments; take some responsibility for the learning of others; and practice skills of framing questions and interpreting questions.

SIZE OF GROUP

A group of ten or more is needed.

MATERIALS NEEDED

None.

TIME REQUIRED

Approximately 25 minutes are required as a minimum.

ADVANCE PREPARATION

This should take about five minutes of class time.

1. Give the students the reading assignment for the next class session.

2. Ask each person to bring to the next session two substantive, important questions, derived from the assigned material, for consideration by the class members.

3. Inform the class that at that (next) session you will identify a committee of four students to help process the questions raised by the class members.

PROCESS

This will take about 25 minutes, or more.

1. At the commencement of the class session, identify a four-person committee.

2. The class members not on the committee are to present (in some order, sequence) questions to the committee.

3. Out loud, for all to hear, the committee discusses the question and achieves some consensus on a response which the committee communicates to the class. Showmanship is not the goal here, so attempts at "acting" should be negatively reinforced in a tactful way.

4. Reality check. After each such response, or, after all questions have been processed, the instructor asks questioners/others to reflect on the adequacy of response. If all questions are first processed by the committee prior to reality check, the instructor will need to record all questions and responses.

5. The instructor has the obvious responsibility of correcting errors, misinformation, misinterpretations, etc., as the process unfolds.

11

Crossfire Panel

PURPOSE

The purpose is to identify information, viewpoints, attitudes, etc., in reference to some topic or topics which are meaningful in the context of the course or program. Communication skills enhancement is also important.

SIZE OF GROUP

The group can range from 20 all the way to 200.

MATERIALS NEEDED

None.

TIME REQUIRED

Approximately 60 minutes.

ADVANCE PREPARATION

No more than 25 minutes.

1. Instructor explains the process (below) and ground-rules.

2. The fundamental topic is identified (students and instructor may negotiate this). The topic should be significant in the context of the course (e.g., "pro-choice/pro-

life"; U.S. intervention in Central America; benefit of capital gains taxation).

3. The panel members are identified: two to address one side of the issue; two to address an opposing side. Instructor will be moderator.

4. Format, ground-rules should be negotiated.

5. The panel members should have at least two weeks to prepare their material. The opposing sides will each have to prepare a team-like integration of material.

PROCESS

This will take approximately 60 minutes.

1. Arrange the room so the four panelists are seated in front of the class and all members can see them. The panelists are seated such that opposing views are alternated (pro,con,pro,con) so as to complicate the us-them posture. The instructor is seated off to the side, but, in front, and he or she moderates as needed; the instructor opens by introducing the panelists (5 min.)

2. Each side has 5 minutes to make opening remarks concerning its position. (10 min.)

3. Discussion. The four members discuss the issues with the intent to inform others of the correctness and appropriateness of their position relative to the information researched. (20 to 25 min.) The audience stays out of it. This part of the activity may require some intervention/control (moderating) on the part of the instructor.

4. Questioning. For clarification purposes only, the audience (class) may ask questions of any of the panel members—no evaluation, side-taking, etc., only questions. (10 min.)

5. Audience Discussion. The instructor leads a discussion with class members. Panelists observe. The purpose of the discussion should be to achieve some general conclusions regarding the topic. (15 min.)

VARIATIONS

One may vary step No. 5 considerably, depending on course content, needs of the group, etc.

Suggested Seating Arrangement

```
                                    Pro
                                    Con
              Instructor
                                    Pro
                                    Con
XXXXXXXXXXXXXXXXXXXXXXXXXXXXXXXXXXXXXXXXXXXXXXX
XXXXXXXXXXXXXXXXXXXXXXXXXXXXXXXXXXXXXXXXXXXXXXX
XXXXXXXXXXXXXXXXXXXXXXXXXXXXXXXXXXXXXXXXXXXXXXX
XXXXXXXXXXXXXXXXXXXXXXXXXXXXXXXXXXXXXXXXXXXXXXX
XXXXXXXXXXXX     AUDIENCE     XXXXXXXXXXXX
XXXXXXXXXXXXXXXXXXXXXXXXXXXXXXXXXXXXXXXXXXXXXXX
XXXXXXXXXXXXXXXXXXXXXXXXXXXXXXXXXXXXXXXXXXXXXXX
XXXXXXXXXXXXXXXXXXXXXXXXXXXXXXXXXXXXXXXXXXXXXXX
```

12

Debate with Teams

PURPOSE

The purposes are to have students: research a topic of interest; develop a presentation strategy; plan for effective use of communication skills; and practice competing.

SIZE OF GROUP

The group should have at least 12 persons.

MATERIALS NEEDED

The materials needed are two small tables (4-6 feet each), four chairs, and normal classroom furniture.

TIME REQUIRED

Approximately 70 minutes.

ADVANCE PREPARATION

1. Topics are to be identified. Let the class in on this. While highly volatile topics (e.g., "pro-choice/pro-life") might be suitable, it is probably desirable to identify topics relevant to the course for which a "correct" answer is not easily determined.

2. The debate consists of two, two-person teams with each team taking a position (pro/con). These choices can be negotiated, or the instructor can make the assignment.

3. The instructor will be moderator for the debate. This will require some planning and forethought.

4. The debate teams prepare for their debate in terms of research. The content or body of relevant information to be given others is not to consume more than 10 minutes.

PROCESS

This will take approximately 70 minutes.

1. Arrange the two teams in front of the class with each team at a table with notes and other materials. Tables are placed in a relaxed, inverted "V" shape, and moderator is seated between the tables. (3 minutes)

2. Moderator introduces the topic and the team members, and re-introduces the basic ground-rules (order of presentation, sequence of events), etc. (5 minutes)

3. Each team member, in alternation between teams, gives no more than a 5-minute presentation (pro or con) based on the research done and strategy chosen. (20 minutes)

4. Following the presentation of this prepared material, a maximum of 15 minutes is allowed for a give-and-take question/response session on the issues and information previously identified. This is where the moderator will need to perform monitoring duties, as needed.

5. Clarification/elaboration. Members of the class may ask questions or points of clarification, etc., of the various team members. No valuing or evaluation is to be per-

mitted—only points of information. This is limited to 5 minutes.

6. Break. The class gets a stretch of 5-8 minutes; the teams confer to identify the key points they wish to make in final summation.

7. Summation. Each team makes a 3 minute summation of its position to the class. (6 minutes)

8. Payoff. (This can be optional). Each class member has a total of 100 points to allocate between the two teams. First, each class member lists on a sheet of paper those features and aspects of the presentation that were most effective in shaping his/her learning. Then, points are awarded to the teams on the basis of an evaluation of the quality of the work done. The instructor collects the papers and, at a later time, gives the debaters their "scores." If necessary, the information is used in the course grading system.

Suggested Seating Arrangement

Instructor

Team   **Team**

XXXXXXXXXXXXXXXXXXXXXXXXXXXXXXXXXXXXXXXXXXXXXX
XXXXXXXXXXXXXXXXXXXXXXXXXXXXXXXXXXXXXXXXXXXXXX
XXXXXXXXXXXXXXXXXXXXXXXXXXXXXXXXXXXXXXXXXXXXXX
XXXXXXXXXXXXXXXXXXXXXXXXXXXXXXXXXXXXXXXXXXXXXX
XXXXXXXXXXXXXX AUDIENCE XXXXXXXXXXXXXX
XXXXXXXXXXXXXXXXXXXXXXXXXXXXXXXXXXXXXXXXXXXXXX
XXXXXXXXXXXXXXXXXXXXXXXXXXXXXXXXXXXXXXXXXXXXXX

13

Focused Dialogue

PURPOSE

The purposes of the activity are to have students: prepare independently/jointly for a brief educational presentation; concentrate on their communication and interpersonal skills; and anticipate the learning needs of others. This is *not* a debate.

SIZE OF GROUP

The group should number at least 10.

MATERIALS NEEDED

The only materials needed are the modest notes required by the two persons in the dialogue.

TIME REQUIRED

Approximately 45 minutes are required.

ADVANCE PREPARATION

1. Dialogue topics are identified. This can be done by the instructor, or negotiated with the class.

2. Students, in pairs, are assigned or choose topics. Note: This activity requires only one pair of students and a

single topic; however, many topics and pairs of students can be identified so that one such dialogue occurs in each of several class sessions.

3. The pairs of students, individually and jointly, plan to research their topic, and prepare to conduct a 20-minute dialogue (not a debate, but see below) on what they have learned in order that they may significantly extend the knowledge of the class members regarding the topic in question.

PROCESS

This takes about 45 minutes.

1. Arrange the room for the dialogue; instructor introduces the two persons in dialogue and the topic. (5 minutes)

2. Dialogue. This should take no more than 20 minutes. The students in dialogue have discretion over the methods, means, etc., they use to achieve their objectives. Little structure need be given them unless this is a graded activity, in which case ground-rules/grade criteria must be identified well in advance.

3. Open Discussion. Following the dialogue, members of the class can raise questions and comments relating to the content of the dialogue; interpretations made; intent of the team, etc. Class members are encouraged to inform the dialogue team what were the most significant things learned. (15-20 minutes)

4. Summary. Instructor-led. It can focus on the effectiveness of the session, questions still unanswered, etc. (5 minutes)

VARIATIONS

1. The dialogue pairs could be focused on the same topic but in a debate format.

2. It is desirable to encourage class members to have a voice in decisions on pair composition and topics from which to choose.

14

Interviewing the Instructor*

PURPOSE

The purposes of this approach are to: lessen student anxiety regarding involvement in a new course; provide for some introductory and socialization experiences for students; and, most importantly, to engage students in meaningful dialogue and learning regarding the nature, purpose, and performance requirements of the course. For the instructor, solely, there are opportunities to learn of the level of sophistication of the students; to learn of the risks they are willing to take; and to engage in a different, novel class opening.

SIZE OF GROUP

At least 12 persons are required for this activity.

MATERIALS NEEDED

The course syllabus or guide and related materials.

TIME REQUIRED

Approximately 90 to 100 minutes of class time are needed.

*Adapted from Serey, Timothy T. 1987. Interviewing the professor: An alternative to the drudgery of the first class. *The Organizational Behavior Teaching Review*, 12 (2): 111-114.

ADVANCE PREPARATION

None.

PROCESS

1. At the very beginning of the class session, distribute copies of the syllabus, course guide, etc., to all of the students and ask them to read the material before the class starts. Put this message on the board, too.

2. Shortly after the class members all quietly begin to read the material, inform them that they should make some notes about any part of the material for which they have a question. Inform them that they have a total of 20 minutes to read the material and note their questions.

3. Next, the class is divided into small groups of at least four persons per group. Each of the groups is to select/elect a representative; the group of representatives is to interview the instructor based on the questions the individual groups generated. The group discussions should be limited to 25 minutes.

4. The representatives are asked to meet shortly and decide how to arrange the room, themselves, etc., physically, for the interview. This should take only a few minutes; the rest of the class members can have a short break/stretch.

5. Interview. Depending on a number of factors (the course, the students, the number of students' questions, etc.) this activity could take from 25-45 minutes. Any question is "fair game" as long as the question has some bearing on the course. This interview presents an excellent opportunity for the instructor to model various behaviors.

6. When the questions conclude on the part of the representatives, the instructor might open the floor to anyone to raise additional questions or comments.

7. Finally, and, at the option of the instructor, the question may be posed to the class: "Why do you suppose I used this activity to begin the class?" The responses to this question will be varied and will provide an opportunity to reinforce a number of behaviors and ideas.

15

Lecture Reaction Panel

PURPOSE

The purposes of this approach are to have students attend closely to important lecture material, create a discussion environment which they maintain, and practice communication skills.

SIZE OF GROUP

At least 15 individuals should participate in this approach.

MATERIALS NEEDED

None.

TIME REQUIRED

At least one hour is required for this approach.

ADVANCE PREPARATION

None.

PROCESS

1. The instructor identifies a Reaction Panel of students. The panel should be of from three to five students, and they should be seated to the side, facing (angle) the instructor and class members. (5 minutes)

2. The instructor gives the panel their task, namely, they are to be highly attentive to the lecture, ask questions, if necessary, etc., and following the lecture they are to collaborate to prepare a brief summary of the most important features of the lecture for disclosure to the class members. All of this does not absolve other class members from attending to the lecture. (5 minutes)

3. Lecture by instructor. This should be no more than 25 minutes.

4. The Reaction Panel has ten minutes to prepare the summary/reactions. The rest of the class has a break/stretch.

5. The summary is presented by the panel. Questions are encouraged from class members and the instructor. The instructor can use the opportunity to clarify, reinforce, correct, etc., responses.

Seating Arrangement
Lecture Reaction Panel

                                        P
                                        A
Instructor   N
                                        E
                                        L

XXXXXXXXXXXXXXXXXXXXXXXXXXXXXXXXXXXXXXXXXXXXX
XXXXXXXXXXXXXXXXXXXXXXXXXXXXXXXXXXXXXXXXXXXXX
XXXXXXXXXXXXX AUDIENCE XXXXXXXXXXXXX
XXXXXXXXXXXXXXXXXXXXXXXXXXXXXXXXXXXXXXXXXXXXX
XXXXXXXXXXXXXXXXXXXXXXXXXXXXXXXXXXXXXXXXXXXXX

16

Question Sharing

PURPOSE

This activity will involve students more thoroughly in their reading assignments and will enhance their communication skills.

SIZE OF GROUP

At least five participants are needed.

MATERIALS NEEDED

None.

TIME REQUIRED

Approximately 40 or more minutes are required.

ADVANCE PREPARATION

This takes about 5 minutes of class time:

1. The instructor gives the group the reading assignment for the next class session.

2. Each student is asked to bring to class two substantive and important questions to ask the class.

PROCESS

Approximately 40 minutes are needed:

1. At the commencement of the class session, or at some appropriate time in the class session, following advance preparation, above, ask students (in-turn, randomly, etc.) to pose their best question to the class.

2. The class members are to respond to the questions. The instructor moderates, as needed.

3. When responses to a given question terminate, the instructor can ask for a "reality check." That is, ask the group if anything else need be said. Ask if they are satisfied with the answers. If there is a gap, poor interpretation, misinformation, etc., the instructor can respond at this point.

4. Proceed as time permits to address as many questions as possible.

Note: This activity, if properly managed, can take the place of or augment a lecture on the material in question.

17

Student Expectations

PURPOSE

The purposes of this activity are to have students: (1) think about and articulate their learning needs; (2) express their fundamental expectations about a course; and (3) express some of their values regarding quality of instruction.

SIZE OF GROUP

With a class of more than 35 students it may be desirable to have students work together in small teams (see Process, step 4b).

MATERIALS NEEDED

Worksheet, see below.

TIME REQUIRED

Depending on the use of teams and amount of discussion generated, the time needed for the activity can range from 25 minutes to 45 minutes.

ADVANCE PREPARATION

A worksheet (see below) must be prepared for distribution to the students.

PROCESS

1. Announce to the students that you want to obtain some information and suggestions from them that could help in setting the stage for the course and could also help in identifying some things that are important to them. This activity provides an opportunity for the instructor and the students to learn something about expectations.

2. Inform students that the head of Herman Miller, furniture manufacturers, Mr. Max DePree (see DePree, M. 1989. *Leadership is an art*, N.Y., N.Y., Doubleday), uses some questions which he has found to be particularly effective with his employees in performance appraisals and in establishing dialogue and focus regarding expectations. We will use some of these questions (as modified) to assist us.

3. Give each student a copy of the worksheet (below) with the three questions and ask them to answer the questions in the next ten minutes.

a. What are a few of the things you need most and expect most from the instructor?

b. If you were "in my shoes" on what key area or matter would you focus?

c. What two things should we do to work toward being a great class?

4a. If there are fewer than 35 students, the instructor could ask each one to respond, aloud, in turn, for each of the three questions. As the students respond, the instructor places key words from their responses on the board.

4b. If there are more than 35 students, the instructor may group them in teams of five students. The teams are asked to compare their responses and on a new "team" worksheet prepare a team response that is representative of their views. This activity should be limited to about 15 minutes. Then, as in 4a, above, the teams respond to the instructor with the team information. Individual students are to submit their worksheets to the instructor after class.

5. The instructor leads a discussion regarding the content of the responses (clusters of similar responses, trends, patterns). Opportunities should be given for students to explain and clarify their meanings and intentions.

6. The instructor should collect all the worksheets. Outside of class, the instructor could examine the individual worksheets for any of a variety of purposes (quality of self-expression, articulateness, word fluency, and the like); and decide how else the information may be used to further the aims of the course as well as respond to the needs and expectations that the students have revealed.

Expectations Worksheet

Name:_____

To help all of us gain a better knowledge of and understanding of the expectations we bring to the course, I'm asking you to respond, carefully, to the three questions, below. For each question write down what is really important to you. You should finish this in about 10 minutes or less.

1. What are a few of the things you expect most and need most from the instructor?

2. If you were "in my shoes" on what key area or matter would you focus?

3. What two things should we do to work toward being a great class?

18

Symposium with Critique

PURPOSE

The purposes are to have students research topics and prepare information and analysis for dissemination; prepare for effective communication; and respond to evaluation and criticism. Focus is not limited to information attainment, as communication skills are considered of importance.

SIZE OF GROUP

From 15 to 150. It is most effective, though, if the group has under 40 members.

MATERIALS NEEDED

The only materials needed are those required by the lead participants (see below).

TIME REQUIRED

Approximately 90 minutes.

ADVANCE PREPARATION

In no more then 20 minutes:

1. Instructor assigns/negotiates the topics to be investigated (four to five students) by the lead participants.

2. Instructor identifies the students (critique group) who will formally react to student presentation of topic information.

3. Instructor sets the class session in which the symposium will occur.

PROCESS

This will take approximately 90 minutes.

1. Arrange the room for the symposium (5 minutes); see next page.

2. Instructor introduces the individual presenters. In turn, each of the four or five lead participants presents information on the topic he/she researched according to whatever guidelines were established in advance. Time limit per each participant is 7 minutes (35 min. total).

3. During the symposium, the critique group (N=4) takes notes, forms questions, and prepares evaluative comments regarding what was done, explained, etc.

4. Following the symposium, the critique group meets privately to discuss what matters should be addressed in the follow-up; which of them should address the various matters, etc. (15 min.) At the same time, all other students should be instructed to prepare a brief statement of what was learned that is of greatest importance to them, individually.

5. Follow-up. The critique group poses questions and evaluative remarks to the lead group members who, of course, are expected to respond. (10-15 min.)

6. Open Forum. When the critique group has concluded, the floor is open to the whole group for questions, observations, comments. (10-15 min.)

7. Summary. The instructor gives a brief summary of what took place, information uncovered, etc., and invites student comment as to the value and effectiveness of the symposium relative to goals. (10 min.)

VARIATIONS

All class members could be required to participate in either lead or critique roles (or both) over the duration of the course.

Suggested Arrangement

Presenters   Critique Group

Remainder of Class
XXXXXXXXXXXXXXXXXXXXXXXXXXXXXXXXXXXXXXXXX
XXXXXXXXXXXXXXXXXXXXXXXXXXXXXXXXXXXXXXXXX

Instructor

Part Three

Formats to Enhance Cognitive and Managerial Skills

19

Background Knowledge Probes*

PURPOSE

These knowledge probes are sets of direct, interrelated questions prepared by the instructor for use at the beginning of a course or at any time during a course, prefatory to the commencement of some new topic. The sampling of background knowledge allows students to take stock of what they already know; and it assists instructors to know what the students bring to the class as well as where the substantive gaps are regarding what is known and what needs to be known about the topic. Also, the information obtained may help the instructor better plan, revise, etc., the instruction for the course.

SIZE OF GROUP

Depending on the number of questions used and complexity of questions, it is not unreasonable to assume that as many as 50 to 80 students could participate in this activity.

MATERIALS NEEDED

The materials needed are copies of the list of questions prepared by the instructor.

*Adapted from Cross, K. Patricia, and Angelo, Thomas A. (1988). *Classroom assessment techniques*, University of Michigan, National Center for Research to Improve Postsecondary Teaching and Learning: 30-32.

TIME REQUIRED

The initial iteration of this activity will require approximately 60 to 90 minutes of class time and up to several hours of the instructor's time to review and analyze responses.

ADVANCE PREPARATION

Prior to the introduction of some substantive new topic or subject in the course, anticipate what the students may already know about the topic/subject.

In jargon-free, direct, simple language compose four to six carefully worded questions that will probe the existing knowledge of the students regarding the topic/subject. By way of example, here are some Background Knowledge Probes for a topic in a course on Behavior in Complex Organizations:

> Example: Managers and supervisors often have to work with groups of individuals (employees), who are part of some regular work unit, department, or crew. These employees are people who: normally see each other each day at work, do some of the same jobs, help each other, and are located in relatively close proximity to one another at work.

a. What does *cohesive* mean regarding the work group?
b. What are the most important aspects of cohesiveness for the work group?
c. What is the relationship of the cohesiveness of the group and work group productivity, functioning, and effectiveness?
d. Suppose a work group which you manage or supervise exhibits a high degree of cohesiveness. What kinds of behavior would be representative of this group? Why?

PROCESS

1. At the appropriate place in the course, either write the questions on the board or give the students a page with the questions.

2. Ask the students to compose short paragraph responses to each of the questions. Approximately four to five sentences for each question should be sufficient. It is important to inform the students that their responses will be carefully reviewed but that the work will not be graded. Students should be given from 5-8 minutes, per question, for preparation of a written response.

3. Have the students hand in their papers and then form them into small groups to discuss the questions and prepare mutually acceptable responses. This activity is for purposes of sharing information, biases, assumptions, and points of view.

4. The instructor will need to review the answers to the questions and eventually make some determinations regarding what is known and not known, etc. One approach for getting started is to sort the responses for each question as follows:

s = significant background knowledge
l = little background knowledge
n = no background knowledge
e = erroneous background knowledge

5. On the basis of the results of such categorization and analysis of the responses, the instructor is able to make decisions regarding instruction in the topic area for a variety of purposes.

Option: Following instruction in the topic area, the instructor may wish to use all or some of the questions (above) in an examination to determine pre/post instruction changes in student learning.

20

Educating the Consumer

PURPOSE

The purposes of this approach are to: increase student responsibility for learning, create interest in assigned material, and integrate reinforcement with performance.

SIZE OF GROUP

There should be at least eight persons if the task is undertaken at the individual leader level; at least 16 if the task is undertaken at the small group level.

MATERIALS NEEDED

A quiz or examination prepared by the instructor.

TIME REQUIRED

This depends on the quantity and complexity of the material. Approximately one hour should be sufficient.

ADVANCE PREPARATION

1. Some reasonable amount (a text chapter?) of course material is assigned to a student or a small group (3 or 4, no larger) of students.

2. Given sufficient advance notice, the content/material is to be taught to the class by the student(s) for the students. The "teacher(s)" are to decide what and how to best do this. The instructor could serve as a resource person.

3. Independent of class contact, the instructor prepares a quiz or examination based on the material in question.

PROCESS

1. The student(s) and the topic/material assigned are introduced by the instructor. (3 minutes)

2. The student indicates what he/she is going to do: how the presentation is structured and organized, etc. (4 minutes)

3. The material is then taught by the student using methods, materials, devices, etc., deemed important to the task. Questions and comments are to be encouraged. "Looking good" really isn't important—effective presentation is important.

4. When the teaching concludes and before the quiz/examination is given to class members (not the presenters), the instructor offers to answer questions, provide interpretations, correct any misinformation, etc.

5. The quiz/examination is given. This work does not have to be heavily weighted for the eventual course grade. That is, one such quiz may not count too much; however, several quizzes, additively, may account for a substantial portion of the course grade.

6. Following the class session, the quiz/examination is graded. The class average grade is awarded to the "teacher" (presenter) of the material. All students know this in advance. Motivationally, it is in one's best

interest to be an effective teacher, as one's success is inextricably tied to the success of the consumers. Not surprisingly, more than a few students are *not* going to like this feature!

21

The Forum

PURPOSE

The purposes of this approach are to have students attend closely to an assigned, out-of-class task (homework?), practice communication skills, and reinforce learning.

SIZE OF GROUP

At least 12 students are needed for this approach to insure some diversity of responses.

MATERIALS NEEDED

None.

TIME REQUIRED

This approach can be conducted in one hour or less.

ADVANCE PREPARATION

The following requires about five minutes of class time:

1. The instructor makes an assignment such as required reading, or observation of some event, TV show, film, etc.

2. The expectation announced is that all students come to class prepared to addresss, out-loud, some important

aspect of what was learned as a result of the assignment.

PROCESS

1. The instructor presents his/her goals and objectives for the Forum. This does not need to be too complex; rather, some boundaries and parameters are probably sufficient. (5 minutes)

2. Any ground-rules (time limits, order, sequence, etc.) the instructor wants to be in place should be presented. (5 minutes)

3. Forum. With respect to the assignment, all class members are expected to contribute their reactions, observations, interpretations, etc., within the general framework of the goals and objectives. If they stray too far, the instructor must moderate. Also, those who hang back should be called on for their contributions. When a lull occurs, the instructor might suggest that if he/she were to prepare an examination or quiz, what would be the areas that should be included on the examination, and why include them? (40 minutes)

4. Summary. The instructor should conduct a brief summary of the substantive contributions made by the class members. This can serve to reinforce important aspects of the assignment.

22

Idea Exploration*

PURPOSE

The purpose of this format is to have students interact in a systematic approach to the generation and exploration of ideas. Group interaction is required as well as writing and clarification skills. Also, the method provides equal opportunity for student participation.

SIZE OF GROUP

There are no restrictions on the maximum size of the group; however, the group should have ten to twelve participants as a minimum.

MATERIALS NEEDED

Students need pads and pens. Also needed in the classroom are newsprint or flip-chart pad, felt-tipped pens (black, green, red), and masking tape.

TIME REQUIRED

Depending on the complexity and ambiguity of the issues to be discussed, the time needed for the activity typically ranges from one to two hours. One hour is often sufficient.

*Adapted from Moore, Carl M. 1987. *Group techniques for idea building.* Beverly Hills, CA.: Sage Publications. See Chapter 3, Idea Writing.

ADVANCE PREPARATION

Prior to the meeting in which the format is applied, the instructor will need to develop stimulus questions. One tactic to use is to give only one stimulus question to the entire group. All participants respond to the same question. A second tactic is to prepare from three to five stimulus questions and: (a) assign them to individuals or groups or (b) have participants choose questions on which to work. The multiple-question tactic creates greater opportunities for individual choice/involvement; however, it is a bit more difficult for the instructor to coordinate.

Here are some sample stimulus questions from different disciplines:

1. What can be done in West County to reduce the rate of illiteracy? (Education)

2. How can local governments establish priorities for initiatives in economic development? (Political Science)

3. How can the quality of pre-natal care be enhanced in the general public? (Health, Nursing)

PROCESS

1. Moore (1987) suggests that these things be presented to the participants:
a. stress the importance of the task;
b. explain how the results will be used;
c. outline the basic steps of the process:
   (1) small working groups of from four to seven persons are formed;
   (2) each person prepares a written response to a stimulus question on a pad;
   (3) pads with responses are placed in the middle of the small group;
   (4) each person reacts, in writing, on the pad of each other member of the small group;

(5) following the recording of the written comments, each participant reads, aloud, the
comments written in response to his/her
ideas; discussion takes place and the group
summarizes its findings and conclusions on
newsprint; and,

d. ask for questions, etc.

2. Divide the entire group into small groups of from four
to seven members. It is desirable to create heterogeneous
groups. Create small groups with diversity in gender, age, experience, and if possible, ability. Each group is to have a
leader/timekeeper.

3. The instructor provides (on chalkboard, newsprint, etc.)
the stimulus question(s). Participants are to write their names
on the top of the page (on the pad) and stimulus question immediately below the name. Moore (1987) suggests use of an
instruction page (see at the end of this format) when the number of participants is large.

4. Each participant is to prepare in legible form a response
to the stimulus question. This response should take no more
than ten minutes to prepare.

5. After these initial responses are prepared, pads are
placed in the center of the table. Each member, in writing, responds, in turn, on each pad (save his/her own pad). The response may take any form (e.g., criticism, questioning, support, elaboration, provide suggestions, and the like). This
portion of the activity should take no more than 15 minutes.

6. Analysis. Still operating as a small group, each member
reads aloud the comments on their pad for the other members.
Then, the group can discuss the ideas and responses and work
to achieve consensus. A summary of findings and opinions
should be prepared. The summary is placed on newsprint for
display.

7. Summaries are displayed and each group leader reports
the significant elements of his/her group's summary to the
large (whole) group.

8. Finally, the instructor leads a discussion of the whole

group on the ideas and the findings. Open discussion should be encouraged.

Guidesheet for Idea Exploration

Name:_____

Question:

_____

_____

Instructions: Please do the following things:

1. Write your name in the space above.

2. Immediately below these instructions, write your response to the question, above. Work quietly and independently and complete your response within ten minutes.

3. Place your pad in the middle of the group so each of the members may respond to what you have written.

Response:_____

_____

_____

_____

_____

23

Lecture-Focused Teams

PURPOSE

The purposes of this approach are to have students attend closely to important lecture material, reinforce each other's learning, and practice communication skills. This approach is intended to accompany a lecture of the instructor, the content of which is of more than average importance in the scope of the course.

SIZE OF GROUP

At least 12 students should participate in this approach. Maximum size is about 50.

MATERIALS NEEDED

None (optional: large sheets of paper, felt-tipped markers, masking tape—for student reports).

TIME REQUIRED

At least one hour is required, at a minimum, for this approach.

ADVANCE PREPARATION

None, other than the instructor's lecture material.

PROCESS

1. Prior to the lecture, the instructor creates a division of labor among the students so that three to five groups are identified. Each group has particular responsibility for some aspect (interpretation, viewpoint, etc.) of the lecture material. This aspect is their focus. The instructor will need to give this some thought beforehand. The groups should be identified in such a way so as to promote non-homogeneity. (5 minutes)

2. Lecture. The lecture is given/presented. Questions during the lecture are acceptable. (25 minutes)

3. The students work in their groups. Their task is to share ideas, content, interpretations, etc., as per their particular focus so as to prepare a brief summary of key points of the lecture, which is to reinforce the learning of class members. (15 minutes)

4. Teams report their summaries. They may use chalkboard or other means of communicating. The reports may be interrupted with questions, comments, etc. (15-20 minutes)

5. Summary. The instructor may use a summary to reinforce learning and, perhaps, to correct erroneous assumptions.

Part Four

Formats to Enhance Integration and Cooperative-Learning Skills

24

The Action Project*

PURPOSE

The purposes of this approach are to have students seize an opportunity to be creative and to integrate theory and concepts learned with practical applications.

SIZE OF GROUP

There are no constraints on the minimum or maximum size of groups.

MATERIALS NEEDED

None.

TIME REQUIRED

It is difficult to project in-class time needed for this approach; however, the entire process takes place over an eight-to ten-week period.

ADVANCE PREPARATION

There are at least two things that need to be in place prior to discussing the assignment in detail with students.

*Adapted from Whitcomb, Susanne W. 1981. The action project. *Exchange: The Organizational Behavior Teaching Journal*, 7: 39-41.

First, several examples of project topics should be available for sharing with students. Some examples are: creating a constitution and by-laws for a local bicycle club, developing a training manual for a small business, setting up and operating a tutoring program, etc.

Second, a grading system is identified, such as: the project has a total of 100 points, with the points allocated thus:

Proposal ....15 points
Design 25
Descriptions of actions.....................15
Conclusions 15
Theory 10
Spelling, snytax, etc. 10
Discretion of instructor ....10 points
(for exemplary work: detail; thoroughness; clarity of organization, expression, etc.)

PROCESS

1. The project requirements can be announced at the first or second class meeting. The Proposal of the project (Part 1) would be due in week three of the course. The Proposal will tell what the student intends to do, why the project is of importance, what results are anticipated, what persons or groups are involved, and any other important background information.

2. Proposals are checked by the instructor for soundness, relevance, clarity, feasibility, etc. This is an opportunity to help the students sharpen their objectives, to give reinforcement and the like.

3. About one-third of the way through the course, the students submit the Design (Part 2) of the project. The Design details the plans and strategies for action and should include, as a minimum:

a. a list of alternative actions and the top priority action;
b. the details of the specific steps that will be taken, in sequence, within the time allowed;
c. a brief description of an alternative strategy or back-up

plan; and

d. a listing of the resources (human and other) needed for success, and how these resources will be obtained.

The Design is not a binding contract but an estimate, subject to some modification(s).

4. Part 3 is due at the end of the course and has three components:

a. a description of actions actually taken;

b. a set of conclusions, having to do with an evaluation of success, criteria for success, identification of five significant things learned, an assessment of how the project could have been more successful having the knowledge now possessed, and what recommendations are proposed—what should happen now; and,

c. relevant theory and concepts applicable in the circumstances.

Calendar, Suggested, for Action Project

Week 1	Announce the project requirement and its components and details.
Week 3	Students submit project proposal. Instructor reviews proposals.
Week 4	Students receive proposals with comments, suggestions, etc.
Week 6	Students submit design section of the project.
Week N	End of the course. Students submit final project report (descriptions of actions, identification of relevant theory/concepts, and conclusions).

25

Chronology Charting*

PURPOSE

The purposes of this activity are to enable students to: review substantive course material; access major concepts, ideas, authors, etc.; and, better understand and appreciate the evolution of thought in a particular discipline or field.

SIZE OF GROUP

A minimum of 12 students is necessary for this activity to be undertaken by small groups. If the activity is undertaken by individuals working alone, the size of group is of no concern.

MATERIALS NEEDED

Large sheets of newsprint paper, felt-tipped markers, masking tape.

TIME REQUIRED

Approximately one hour is needed for this activity.

---

*Adapted from Lundberg, Craig. 1990. Chronology charting. *Organizational Behavior Teaching Review,* 14(1): 155-156.

ADVANCE PREPARATION

None for the instructor. Students are expected to have read and studied the body of material in questions prior to the class session in which the charting is done.

PROCESS

1. The instructor introduces the activity by explaining to students that it is a method of review; assessing major ideas, concepts, etc., enabling greater understanding and meaning of substantive course material. Further, the activity may provide the instructor with a variety of examination material, and the students, correspondingly, a useful study guide.

2. The students are placed in four-person groups and are instructed to create a chart which lists in a chronological manner the ideas, concepts, models, movements, theories; the respective author(s)/actors; the date of their first citation or mention; and the corresponding page numbers from the text(s). It is assumed that this activity is focused on major portions of a text(s). The list is typically linear over time; however, other unities (schools of thought, etc.) may govern choice of classification.

3. The lists are eventually completed and placed on the large sheets of paper and attached to walls with masking tape.

4. Once the charts are posted, the instructor leads a comparison review. This helps to identify and reinforce salient materials and also assists the students to visualize the importance, etc., granted to some material by their classmates. The review provides the instructor with the opportunity to examine a wide range of topics, and it also provides opportunities for students to pose questions and to gain new interpretations of material.

**Example of a Chronology Chart
(a beginning)**

From a course on Organizations: chart influences on organization design in the 20th Century.

Pre-1900

    The Church

    Military organizations

    Business organizations

After 1900

    Classical organization principles

    Scientific Management

    Human Relations movement

    Neo-classical principles of management

    Leader behavior concepts

    Theory of Bureaucracy

    Decision Theory influences

    Influences of General Systems Theory

    Influences of contingency theories

26

Clarifying Attitudes Design*

PURPOSE

The purposes of this approach are to help students: become more aware of their current attitudes; apprehend a spectrum of alternative attitudes; and help students make choices regarding the soundness of an attitude in a given set of circumstances.

SIZE OF GROUP

About 15 students are required for this approach.

MATERIALS NEEDED

Chalkboard and/or flip-chart.

TIME REQUIRED

For a short list of topics, approximately three hours are required for the activity.

---

*Adapted from Mouton, Jane S., and Blake, Robert R. 1984. *Synergogy*. San Francisco: Jossey-Bass Publishers.

ADVANCE PREPARATION

1. The instructor will have determined what topics will be examined and will have prepared a single page with topics and instructions (see #1, below, for students).

2. An instructor-prepared, multiple-alternative attitudes questionnaire (see #1, below). This questionnaire may be brief; however, it needs to be prepared in advance.

3. Critique survey (optional). See #6, below.

PROCESS

1. Independently, each student is to write a statement that describes the student's attitude toward the topic being examined. For example, suppose the instructor provided all students with this instruction:

Different attitudes are held by different people regarding features of affirmative action programs (AAPs). Write a brief description of your present attitude toward each (assumes there are several) aspect. Responses should be at least one sentence in length. The items are: (1) AAPs contribute to the health and vitality of an organization; (2) AAPs are designed to assist individuals; (3) AAPs serve the interest of all employees.

Then, a multiple-alternative attitude questionnaire on the items (above) is distributed to the students. The alternatives should represent a full range of attitudes toward the topics such as yes/no, positive/negative, sound/unsound, and so forth. Each student is to read all of the alternatives and rank them in decreasing order (n, n-1, n-2, etc.) with the highest ranking given to the choice most similar to one's own attitude. A one (1) would represent the alternative liked least.

Next, the handwritten attitude statement previously written is examined to check on which of the attitude alternatives is closest to the spontaneous expression of attitude prior to examining the written/given alternatives. The student is then to place the item number of the chosen alternative next to his/her written statement.

2. Teams are formed. The instructor forms teams of from 4-6 students. The teams are to be heterogeneous in composition (age, gender, race, experience, ability, etc.). The teams meet to rank the same attitude alternatives; however, this time the governing criterion is the overall validity or soundness of the alternatives. The same ranking scale (n-1, n-2, etc.) is to be used, and the team is to achieve consensus on the rankings. Further, the team members are to examine the differences between actual attitudes and the soundest one.

3. Personal planning. Team members are now ready to discuss how each one wants to change behavior in order to be consistent with the agreed-upon description of soundest attitude. The team recognition of "soundness" can be a powerful reinforcer of behavior change.

4. Shared norms. Representatives from each team report team rankings to the whole class. The instructor records the information on the chalkboard or flip-chart so as to examine similarities and differences. The objective in this stage is to reach a deeper understanding of reasons and teams' conclusions.

5. Re-ranking of attitudes. The team members re-rank the set of attitude alternatives to reflect their present attitudes toward the topic. This ranking is supposed to be independent of the earlier ranking.

6. Critique of teamwork. Each team will spend some time in evaluation and assessment of the performance of the team relative to team functioning, attainment of objectives, sensitivity/helpfulness with member aims, and the like. The instructor can influence this activity by providing a brief questionnaire, checklist, survey, etc., addressing such points as listed in the previous sentence; or, the instructor may give teams complete latitude to conduct their own critique so long as a written summary is provided to the instructor.

27

Cooperative Testing*

PURPOSE

The purposes of this approach are to have students: attend carefully to "must cover" reading material in a course; work individually and collectively on test material taken from the reading; and achieve feedback on their understanding of material, study, strategy, and the like.

SIZE OF GROUP

The size of the group can range from a small group of eight or ten to as many as several hundred students.

MATERIALS NEEDED

Each time this approach is used an examination or quiz will need to be prepared. For classes of 30 or more students it is recommended that the examination consist of objective-type questions. Depending on the scope and complexity of the assigned reading, the examination should reflect instructional objectives.

*Adapted from Kurfiss, J. 1987. The reasoning-centered classroom: Approaches that work. *American Association for Higher Education Bulletin,* March/April: 12-14.

TIME REQUIRED

In general, this approach in a single, simple iteration should require no more than 45-50 minutes of class time. This assumes that students are reasonably well-prepared and the examination consists of about 30 objective questions.

ADVANCE PREPARATION

The instructor will have to prepare an examination as per Materials, above.

PROCESS

1. Reading material (chapters, book, articles, etc.) is assigned to the class and an examination or quiz is also assigned for the next (or some future) class session.

2. At the next class session all students complete the examination and submit their papers to the instructor for grading.

3. Then, the students are placed in heterogeneous groups of from four to six students to re-take the examination. The groups may be permanent groups, or the group personnel can be changed if this approach is used again and again. The students are to discuss examination items and reach consensus on responses to all items. A group examination is then completed and submitted to the instructor for grading.

4. At a later time the instructor grades both the individual examinations and the group examinations. Each student earns two grades, weighted equally, for each examination.

5. Once the examinations are graded, student groups have the option of appealing incorrect answers/responses, in writing. Such appeals, if successful, will require grade adjustments.

This approach provides the instructor with information regarding student understanding of the material in question; it brings into focus the problem areas that may require detailed explanation; it provides some freedom from examining details which students can learn on their own, thereby permitting the instructor to use applications based on the reading and/or to focus more on analysis and synthesis vs. acquisition.

28

Group Investigation*

PURPOSE

The purposes of this cooperative learning approach are to assist students to: be successful achievers in a cognitive sense; learn of the practical utility of team functioning; and, learn, first-hand, of the power and influence of performance interdependence.

SIZE OF GROUP

For this approach the class size should be some multiple of five. A group of 15 students or larger would be desirable. The multiple of five criterion, however, is not an absolute requirement—only a preference.

MATERIALS NEEDED

Chalkboard and/or flip-chart.

TIME REQUIRED

Depending on the magnitude and/or complexity of the topics, etc., this approach will require several hours of class and out-of-class time. In a traditional, 45 clock-hour, semester course, this approach could take as much as 20-25 percent of time available.

*Adapted from Sharan, Y., and Sharan, S. 1990. Group investigation expands cooperative learning. *Educational Leadership*, 47 (4): 17-21

ADVANCE PREPARATION

None.

PROCESS

Group investigation harnesses students' interests and gives them much control over their own learning. The fundamental process contains six stages, and these stages, depending on the calendar of class meetings, etc., could be compressed into one to two weeks or spread over several weeks.

1. Introductory Phase
   a. Identify topic to be investigated and organize students into groups. A topic can start as a question. Multi-faceted topics are best.
   b. Students need to select sub-topics for inquiry. Some ways to do this:
      (1) Each student raises questions he/she would like to investigate—instructor lists on board or flip-chart.
      (2) Buzz-groups meet to list ideas and report to whole class.
      (3) Students write questions they would like to have answered. Place students in progressively larger groups (2-4-8); they compare lists, eliminate duplicates, and compile a single list. Then, move to structure a final list for the class.
   c. All suggestions are made available to the whole class.
   d. Instructor places all questions into some categories; the categories become sub-topics.
   e. Sub-topics are presented to the class; students join the group (limit size) that is studying the sub-topic of his/her choice.
2. Group members formulate a researchable problem and plan their course of action. Members must decide who will study which aspect of the sub-topic. The instructor

can circulate among groups and offer assistance. One group member is the recorder and writes down questions, etc. The instructor may want to provide each group with a worksheet that contains:

Research topic;

Group members;

Roles of members;

What do we want to find out?

What are our resources?

As each group completes these worksheets, the worksheets can be posted for all class members to review.

3. Carry out the investigation. Much of this is done using class time in contrast to having all the work done out of class; or having a major portion of it done out of class. The students gather information, analyze and evaluate data, reach conclusions, and apply their share of new knowledge to "solving" the group's research problem. The instructor meets with each group periodically to discuss progress, problems, agenda, etc.

4. Prepare final report. There must be a final, summative product of the group. It could be an exhibit, a model, a written report, a dramatic presentation, a slide or videotape presentation, etc. As investigations are winding down, and the groups are beginning to wrestle with the final report options, a coordinating committee is formed (member from each group) to discuss options, sequence, formats, and the like. In essence, they need to orchestrate the final reports so as to integrate efforts and not compete with one another.

5. Presentation of final reports. The whole class is assembled for this phase.

6. Evaluation (some choices)

   a. Instructor evaluates the investigation process of a group, itself (e.g., plans, resources used, use of inferences, draw-conclusions, etc.).

   b. Groups can submit questions (say, two or three per group). These questions could become the basis of the final examination. Groups might evaluate responses of classmates to their questions.

c. Have debriefings to discuss what was learned; how students react to the process, etc.

29

Integration Exercise*

PURPOSE

The purposes of this approach are to help students: recognize the panoply of interactions among important (course) areas, attain a structure for understanding the important concepts and theories, and interact with knowledgeable peers regarding interpretations of causes and effects.

SIZE OF GROUP

An appropriate number of students would range from 12 to 50.

MATERIALS NEEDED

The only material that is needed is sufficient copies of the matrix sheet (see below, Advance Preparation).

TIME REQUIRED

Approximately two hours are required for this approach. The work could be divided into two, one-hour segments.

---

*Adapted from Taylor, R.R., Worrell, D., and Watson, W. 1986. The behavioral process integration exercise. *Organizational Behavior Teaching Review*, 10: 120-122.

ADVANCE PREPARATION

The instructor needs to prepare a matrix sheet with four or five significant areas of the course identified on the axes (a 16 or 20 cell matrix). Below are two examples of matrix sheets; one for a course in real estate, and one for a course in organization behavior.

Example 1: Real Estate
Integrated Elements (effects)

	Listings	Law of Agency	Brokerage Services	Advertising
Listing				
Law of Agency				
Brokerage Services				
Advertising				

Example 2: Organization Behavior
Interrelated Elements (effects)

	Perception	Communication	Leadership	Motives	Group Behavior
Perception					
Communication					
Leadership					
Motives					
Group Behavior					

PROCESS

1. Divide the class into small groups of 5 or 6 students, with each group given one of the topic areas.

2. Distribute the copies of the matrix sheet to all students and explain how the process will help them learn to integrate the major areas of the course.

3. The groups are to work as units for no more than 30 minutes. Their task is to identify how their area affects, impacts, etc., the other areas listed in the matrix. For example, how does the law of agency relate to advertising, listings of property, and brokerage services in the real estate business?

4. Reports. Each group, through a primary presenter with assistance from other group members, is to present a review of how its area has an "effect" on the other areas. This report should take no more than 15 minutes per group, and this may include questions/comments from any of the students in the class. In their deliberations and reports, students should be encouraged to make an effort to use concepts, theories, etc., from what had been discussed, studied, used in the course.

5. Summary. Following the reports, and at the option of the instructor, the instructor may lead a brief wind-down segment in which the students volunteer to state how the activity enhanced their knowledge and understanding.

30

Interview by Panel

PURPOSE

The purposes are to have students: learn to research a topic; collaborate on a joint learning task; and, practice communication skills with an audience.

SIZE OF GROUP

The group should number 10 or more.

MATERIALS NEEDED

None.

TIME REQUIRED

Approximately 45 minutes are needed.

ADVANCE PREPARATION

Class time is needed for this — 30 minutes.

1. Topics appropriate to the course are identified. Students are expected to contribute suggestions.

2. A group of three students is identified (could have many groups, many topics over the duration of the course). The students are to research a topic, prepare questions, some background information, etc., and

plan, collaboratively, to conduct a 20-minute interview of the instructor regarding the topic in question.

3. Class members who are not panelists will be expected to write a one- to two-page paper on how the interview activity enhanced their learning.

PROCESS

This will take approximately 45 minutes.

1. Interviewers arrange the furniture, etc., to conduct the interview. One of them introduces the instructor and the interviewers. (5 minutes)

2. Interview. This should take no more than 20 minutes, so the interview will be highly focused and the attention of the class members will be fully engaged.

3. Questions. When the interview has concluded, class members may ask questions of the interviewers and/or the instructor. Depending on the topic, issues raised, interpretations given/perceived, etc., this segment could be a lively part of the activity and one which stimulates learning. (5-15 minutes)

4. Follow-up. As class activity or as a homework assignment, students are to write a paper (see #3 in Advance Preparation).

31

Jigsaw*

PURPOSE

The purposes of this cooperative learning approach are to assist students to: be successful achievers in a cognitive sense; learn of the practical utility of team effort; and learn first-hand of the influence of performance interdependence.

SIZE OF GROUP

The minimum group size is 12.

MATERIALS NEEDED

None.

TIME REQUIRED

This approach will require several hours. The instructor will have to determine total class time given to the activity based on such factors as class maturity, task complexity, availability of resources, and the like.

ADVANCE PREPARATION

None.

*Adapted from Aronson, E., Blaney, N., Stephan, C., Sikes, J., and Snapp, M. 1978. *The jigsaw classroom*. Beverly Hills, CA: Sage Publications.

PROCESS

1. Students are assigned to groups of six members. The groups should be heterogeneous as to gender, age, experience, race, etc.

2. The academic material to be learned (articles, parts of chapters, full chapters, books, etc.) is divided equally, insofar as possible, into five sections.

3. Each team member chooses a section of the material to study. To help protect the group from effects of student absences—two students will share a section of the material. The selections for sharing will be different from group to group.

4. Individual members study their section of material knowing, in advance, that they will be expected to teach what they have learned to others on their team.

5. Members from different teams who have selected the same section of the material meet in "expert" groups to discuss what they have learned and how to best instruct others regarding what has been learned.

6. The students return to their teams and take turns teaching their material to team members.

7. When the groups have completed their within-team instruction, an examination is administered to the class.

8. Following the examination, group members complete an evaluation form to report how each member perceives his/her own performance and the performance of the group.

9. The class goes through a debriefing session in which the examination is carefully reviewed. The instructor has the option finally, to record individual student examination grades; or have the details worked out in advance, to use individual grades to compute a team grade as well.

32

Peer and Individually Mediated Modeling*

PURPOSE

The purposes of this approach are to have students: create models of performance that are clearly identifiable and credible; use modeling activities whereby skills are identified, validated, and practiced; and make use of feedback and encourage self-control. This approach was developed to enhance the learning of core leader and/or manager skills.

SIZE OF GROUP

If the group has more than 40 participants, the instructor cannot attend to critical features of individual student performance.

MATERIALS NEEDED

Newsprint, felt-tipped markers (red, black), and masking tape.

TIME REQUIRED

This approach is labor-intensive. Depending on the size of the student group, the variety of skills to be examined, and the number of iterations of skill practices, the approach requires

*Adapted from Lyons, P. 1991. A social learning paradigm for management education. In *Empowerment in the workplace and classroom.* Proceedings of the Eastern Academy of Management, Hartford, CT.

approximately five hours in-class time and several more hours of homework are required.

ADVANCE PREPARATION

Having understood the components and expected outcomes of this approach, the instructor should identify skills to be learned and practiced. That is, prior to the introduction of this approach to the class, the instructor should identify four or five skills that are compatible with the approach and are clearly related to content and/or focus of the course of study.

PROCESS

1. For the identification of a skill to be learned, practice needs to take place. The instructor may suggest a skill; the instructor and the students may discuss several skills and agree on one of them as a focal point. For purposes of the explication of this lesson format, the skill, *managing a meeting*, is identified.

2. Identification of teams. In this phase, students are placed into teams of from four to five members each. For the initial use of this approach the instructor should identify the teams (membership). Composition of the teams should reflect as much diversity as possible (gender, age, experience, ability, etc.) so as to potentially tap a variety of adaptive competencies.

3. Exploration of skill attributes. Each team, independently using its own agenda for task differentiation, is to perform three tasks, in sequence, as directed by the instructor. These tasks represent an inductive learning strategy.

   (a) From the recollection, beliefs, etc., of the team members, prepare a list of behaviors that are indicative of high quality performance in managing a meeting. For each behavior, at least one supporting statement (reason) must be supplied. A copy of the list is given to the instructor.

(b) Access and summarize material (from books, texts, research literature, etc.) that addresses qualitative and quantitative interpretations of performance of the skill (managing a meeting). The instructor serves as a resource for the teams. A copy of the summary is given to the instructor.

(c) Once steps "(a)" and "(b)" are completed, the instructor asks the teams to examine both the "(a)" and "(b)" lists and reconcile them, by consensus. The product of the reconciliation is a single list which represents the qualitative and quantitative features of the effective management of meetings. A copy of this "(c)" list is given to the instructor.

4. Meeting. The members of all teams are assembled together, and each team presents a report of its list "(c)" of features. Questions for clarification are acceptable. Copies of all "(c)" lists are shared in the entire group. The teams should place the significant features of their findings on newsprint and place the pages on the walls for all participants to view.

5. Script identity. In this phase, the four-member teams are to take their "(c)" lists and modify them, if they wish, based on the new information received (above). Then, the team is to differentiate among the listed behaviors as to which ones are nearly always necessary or required for the effective management of meetings and which ones are of less importance/significance, yet clearly desirable for the effective management of meetings. A copy of this reconstituted list is given to the instructor. All team members are to have a copy of the list. This task represents a deductive learning strategy.

The next phase of this instruction approach has many significant learning objectives and outcomes. Students learn concepts and skills which are applicable in a variety of settings. Memory patterns are sharpened through exploration and testing of cognitions. The learner should integrate, in memory, cognitions and cause-effect relationships. Modeling and practice increase knowledge. They positively influence individual assessment of self-efficacy by building self-belief in capability, receipt of encouragement from valued peers, and by demonstration of strategies for managing complex situations.

6. Practice/evaluation/feedback. Within each team, each member is to model a brief meeting. Each meeting-model should have a different focus. For example: meetings for the purposes of problem solving, scheduling, decision-making, presenting information, and the like. The content of the discussion does not need to be too complex.

For each performance, members are to make some notes and prepare some assessments of the quality of the efforts to manage the meeting. This can be relatively informal, using the list (above) as the starting point for discussion. Hence, the value of the performance and the validity of the contents of the list (or script) are examined.

The instructor may move from team to team and sit in on the performances and on the feedback sessions.

Practice and repetition are important in script development and modeling. Iteration, the next phase, on the surface may appear merely as the means by which all team members have a turn at practice and feedback. However, iteration is much more complex than turn-taking. Basically, it represents a regulatory, goal-directed process which includes opportunities for greater self-awareness, and perceptions of satisfaction and self-efficacy.

7. Iterations. Following each individual member's performance and evaluation, phases 5 and 6 are repeated so all members have the opportunity to perform, etc., and content of the script may be modified.

8. Review. The instructor should lead a discussion with the participants as to the effects of the approach on their learning and functioning. Emphasis should be on the perceived change of their knowledge, their feelings of confidence and competence, and the like.

Peer and Individually Mediated Modeling
Schedule of Events

1. Skill identification

2. Creation of teams

3. Exploration of skill attributes:

    a. Experienced-based input
    b. Expert-based input
    c. Integration of inputs

4. Plenary session—share information

5. Script identification

6. Practice/evaluation/feedback

7. Skill practice sessions (iterations)

8. Review

Sample
PIMM–Worksheet A
Instructor Observations/Checklist

Team Number/Name:_____

Team Members:_____

Team Has Prepared Agenda for the Task:

Comments

_____

_____

_____

Team Generated Performance Indicators:

Comments

_____

_____

_____

Summary of Literature Search:

Comments

_____

_____

_____

List of "Effectiveness" Features (the "(c)" list):

Comments

_____

_____

_____

Script Identity List:

Comments

_____

_____

_____

Comments on Student Performances:

_____

_____

_____

SAMPLE
PIMM–Worksheet B
Team Checklist

1. Creation of Team's Agenda. List the significant components of the team's task.

_____

_____

2. Exploration of Skill Attributes
   a. List behaviors (and rationale) indicative of high quality performance of the skill. All members contribute.

   _____

   _____

   b. Prepare report/summary from literature search. Need division of labor, strategy, time lines, etc.

   _____

   _____

   c. Reconciliation of information and creation of the "(c)" list.

   _____

   _____

3. Preparation of report to class. Need to determine tasks/roles for compilation, preparation of report, delivery of report, etc.

_____

_____

4. Script Identity.

_____

_____

5. Practice.

_____

_____

6. Feedback/evaluation.

_____

_____

33

Performance-Judging Design*

PURPOSE

The purposes of this approach are to enable students to: acquire skills; develop and apply appropriate criteria; evaluate how other students apply the criteria to skill performance, and to use criteria to judge their own performance or product.

SIZE OF GROUP

At least eight students should comprise the group.

MATERIALS NEEDED

Normally, no materials are needed, although for some activities video recording/playback equipment may be required. See Advance Preparation, below.

TIME REQUIRED

This approach will require several hours and may take place over a number of class sessions. There are six steps in the approach.

*Adapted from Mouton, J.S., and Blake, R.R. 1984. *Synergogy.* San Francisco: Jossey-Bass Publishers.

ADVANCE PREPARATION

The instructor will need to prepare materials necessary for enabling the students to know what particular skill is to be developed and to provide some initial external criteria. For example, suppose the skill to be developed is preparation, in writing, of a performance appraisal of an employee. The instructor could provide a set of external criteria (guides) taken from the literature on performance appraisal; and, also, would provide a set of information about a fictional employee, Mr. Schmidlapp, for whom students are to prepare an appraisal. (This example is used below.) Additional trial material will also need to be prepared.

PROCESS

1. Independently, students complete a task that demonstrates their current level of skill. In our example (performance appraisal), students practice the skill using the materials provided by the instructor. Obviously, a different mode would be a role-play, where the student would orally provide the appraisal and the activity could be videotaped.

2. Once all of the students have practiced the skill, they are placed in four-person heterogeneous teams. The teams are to prepare a set of criteria for assessing the skill. The set of criteria is to be thorough, clear, and explicit. Team members are to reach agreement as to the efficacy of the criteria as representative of the performance of a highly skilled person.

3. The instructor provides teams with the external criteria/standards taken from authoritative sources. The teams study and discuss these criteria and use them to expand or otherwise modify the criteria they have developed. Then, all teams are convened to discuss criteria. Each team receives a copy of the other teams' criteria. Through discussion, the class achieves consensus on the final set of criteria.

4. Teams are given information to generate sample performances of the particular skill. Each team member is responsible for one sample. The samples of skill presentations are demonstrated by each team member, in turn. Notes/observa-

tions are recorded and the team then discusses how the sample compares to the established criteria for effectiveness.

5. Evaluation. The team should identify the similarities and differences among all samples and then evaluate the strengths and needs of each relative to the criteria. This evaluation must be made specific and clear so the student will understand his/her sample's strengths and needs. The student is to summarize, in writing, the team's conclusions (consensus). No one should leave this phase of the work until all possess a clear understanding of their performance.

6. A second performance. A new, more difficult/complex assignment is given to each person on the team. The steps given above in Nos. 4 and 5 are repeated. Perhaps a third or fourth trial will be necessary for students to attain the desired level of skill.

Schedule of Events
Performance Judging Design

1. Task performance to demonstrate current level of skills.
2. Teams formation.
3. Identification of criteria for assessing skill performance.
4. Group consensus achieved on skill criteria.
5. Infusion of external criteria.
6. Final skill performance criteria established.
7. Skills are practiced, assessed.
8. Performances are collectively assessed.

34

The Student-Powered Course*

PURPOSE

The purposes of the approach are to have students exhibit initiative, creativity, and self-direction, and to eschew passivity and "follower-ship." Note: This approach is especially useful in courses where interpersonal behavior, group dynamics, and decision-making are important aspects. The approach is quite flexible and subject to modification/embellishment, and withdrawal of some of the freedoms suggested. It requires much initiative and energy on the part of students and much risk-taking and openness on the part of the instructor.

SIZE OF GROUP

At least 12 students should be members of the group.

MATERIALS NEEDED

It is assumed that some body of material (textbooks, articles, etc.) has been identified as being important or essential to the course; however, no specially-prepared materials are required to implement the approach.

*Adapted from Weil, Jeffrey L. 1988. Management experientially taught. *Organizational Behavior Teaching Review*, 12 (3): 54-61.

TIME REQUIRED

The format-as-approach consumes the entire course (assumes a traditional, 3-credit, semester-long course); however, the fundamental decision-making activity consumes from four to five class hours. In the context given, the decision-making activity (student-led) will take about 10 percent of the class time allowed for the course.

ADVANCE PREPARATION

Mentally, the instructor is prepared to delegate the management of the operation of the course to the students. Instructor intervention should be minimal, and the instructor must be able to carefully articulate the general standards of the school, the discipline, etc., which are not to be violated.

PROCESS

1. The instructor informs the students that they will find the course depends on a fundamental role-reversal. That is, students are to assume roles of instructor/leader and, in essence, to take the stage. The instructor will serve as a resource person, a reflector of ideas, and in some cases, a coach. The final authority for course content, processes, grading, and policy is retained by the instructor.

2. The students are further informed that planning, organization, directing, and controlling of the course are their responsibilities. The purpose of this approach is to permit them to initiate, create, lead, and use the knowledge and intellect they possess in a self-directed way. They are in a partnership with the instructor.

3. Task. The initial task for the class is to develop a detailed set of responses to three basic questions:

a. What do we want to do in the course?

b. Why do you want to do it?

c. How do you want to do it?

This is a very big order for most students. They do not normally have such responsibility: they have no pre-determined agenda or structure. It may require several hours for them to put in writing the details regarding what topics, etc., should be included, identification of required behavior, what should be graded, etc.

4. Depending on the progress of the group, its size, content, etc., the instructor may wish to help by suggesting some standards for facilitating the management of the task. For example, it may be wise to have a committee for coordination and record-keeping; another for identifying important content/topics; another for evaluation/grading, and so on. If students will be grading other students, it may be desirable to form a "grievance committee."

5. As the students near completion of the deliberations regarding the three questions, one of the things that must be done in this approach is the preparation of the course contract (a committee can work on this, too). The contract would include all of the substantive definitions, features, policy on attendance, course performance requirements, and grading standards. All students are expected to sign the contract.

6. The course gets under way as designed.

**Areas of Course/Instruction Students
Should Consider in
the Student-Powered Course**

Course objectives

Individual student objectives

Scope of the course content

Evaluation and assessment

Calendar

Activities

Organization

Leadership

Policy questions regarding such things as:

   Grading Standards
   Attendance
   Late Work

Choice of materials

Other?

35

Student Teams Achievement Division*

PURPOSE

The purposes of this cooperative learning approach are to assist students to: be successful achievers in a cognitive sense; learn of the practical utility of team effort; learn first-hand of the influence of performance interdependence.

SIZE OF GROUP

The minimum group size is twelve.

MATERIALS NEEDED

The instructor will need to have prepared in advance a set of questions (short-answer, multiple-choice, true-false, etc.) keyed to presentation-lecture material. In essence this is a worksheet. An examination will also need to be prepared.

TIME REQUIRED

This approach will require from two to six hours. The instructor will need to determine total class time given to the activity based on factors such as: complexity of material, volume of the material, student readiness, complexity of evaluation, etc.

*Adapted from Slavin, Robert E. 1983. *Cooperative learning*. New York: Longman.

ADVANCE PREPARATION

See "Materials," above.

PROCESS

1. Students are assigned to groups of four to five members. The group should be heterogeneous as to gender, age, ability, race, etc.

2. The instructor presents a prepared lecture to the class. Because of the time and energy consumed in this overall approach, the instructor may want to focus this particular lecture on material that is of great importance relative to course/program goals.

3. Following the lecture, the students assemble as teams and are given the questions, etc. (see Materials) as a worksheet. The students are to work collaboratively to answer the questions, quiz one another, and reach general consensus on answers to all of the questions presented.

4. The instructor then goes over the questions with the whole class so that correct answers are determined. Then, the groups re-convene to discuss their progress, etc. This may not take too long.

5. An examination or quiz is given to all students, individually, and the papers are collected.

6. Scoring of the examination/quiz. Individuals' examination grades are added to give a team score. Individual contributions of a student are calculated by the excess of a given student's score over the team (or class) average score. Perfect papers automatically earn an additional 10 points (bonus). Further, if a base score has been established (say, three points below the class average), a student may earn bonus points for scores above the base. This last item is optional. In essence, we have an individual and group reinforcement system in place to reward performance interdependence and individual effort.

Glossary

ACTIVE LISTENING—the appropriate provision of feedback that facilitates the achievement of meaning among communicators.

AUTONOMOUS TASK GROUPS—small task groups that have responsibility for completion of a specific task.

BRAINSTORMING—a method of problem-solving in which all members of a group spontaneously and freely contribute ideas.

CHANGE AGENT—one who facilitates change in a unit of an organization (a class, in this context).

COALITION—an *ad hoc* alliance formed to influence events.

COGNITION—to know; knowledge gained through perception, reasoning, or intuition.

COLLABORATIVE LEARNING—joint intellectual effort where students and instructor work toward mutually-determined objectives.

COMMUNICATION—a process whereby symbols generated by people are received and responded to by other people.

COMMUNICATION RULES—the definition of the communication process to be used by group/class members.

CONFLICT—disagreements that occur when the correspondence of or aspirations and/or wants of one party or group are not in congruence with the aspirations and/or wants of another party or group.

CONSENSUAL DECISION-MAKING—in a group setting when a decision made reflects the collective opinion of the group.

COOPERATIVE LEARNING—students learn from working together in small groups on intellectual tasks with joint incentives and, possibly, individual incentives.

CRITERIA—standards upon which a judgment is based.

DECISION-MAKING PROCESS—to define the problem; consider and select an alternative; implementation; and follow-up.

DECISION RULES—guidelines that direct a group decision-making process.

DEDUCTION—inference by reasoning from the general to the specific.

EVALUATION—assessment of the consequences of past decisions.

FEEDBACK—in two-way communication, when a receiver responds to the original sender of a communication.

FORMAL GROUP—a group made up of members brought together for the purposes of making decisions and solving problems.

FORUM—an assembly of a group for purpose of open discussion.

GOAL SETTING—the process of setting goals (statements that provide direction for action).

GROUP COHESIVENESS—an atmosphere of closeness and/or attachment that results in a group with a common purpose, values, and attitudes.

GROUP DYNAMICS—the interactions of individuals within a group that affect the functioning and productivity of the group.

IN-BASKET—a problem-solving or priority-setting task where

individuals or small groups respond to a variety of stimuli presented to them.

INDUCTION—to derive general principles from particular instances or facts.

INFORMAL ORGANIZATION—in the classroom setting, the informal or *ad hoc* structure that results from the perceived status and/or power of certain individuals.

INTEGRATE—to make into a whole by bringing all parts together.

LEADERSHIP—to provide structure and/or consideration for others so as to influence their behavior in accomplishing goals you have established.

MATURITY—(in students) a condition of confidence in the knowledge one has and confidence in one's ability to use and attain additional knowledge.

NORMS—standards of behavior expected for an individual within a group.

PANEL—a small group of persons gathered to plan, discuss, or decide something.

PEER EVALUATION—a performance appraisal conducted by classmate(s).

PERCEPTION CHECKING—the investigation or exploration of the content and/or intent of a communication received from another.

PROBLEM FINDING—process of ascertaining the existence of a problem and the scope and components or features of a problem.

ROLE—a part played by one who is acting in a performance.

ROLE AMBIGUITY—a state of uncertainty or confusion regarding the nature of a role.

SYMPOSIUM—a meeting or conference for discussion of some topic.

References

Abelson, R. P. 1981. Psychological status of the script concept. *American Psychologist*, 36: 715-729.

Akin, Gib. 1987. Varieties of managerial learning. *Organizational Dynamics*, Autumn: 36-48.

Albanese, Robert. 1989. Competency-based management education: Three operative and normative issues. *Organizational Behavior Teaching Review*, 14(1): 16-28.

Apps, Jerold W. 1989. Foundations for effective teaching. In Hayes, E. (Ed.) *Effective teaching styles*. San Francisco: Jossey-Bass Publishers.

Aronson, E., Blaney, N., Stephan, C., Sikes, J., and Snapp, M. 1978. *The jigsaw classroom*. Beverly Hills, CA: Sage Publications.

Bandura, Albert. 1986. *Social foundations of thought and action*. Englewood Cliffs, NJ: Prentice-Hall.

Bloom, B.S. *et al*. 1956. *Taxonomy of educational objectives: The classification of educational goals: Handbook I. Cognitive domain*. New York: Longman.

Brandt, Ron. 1990. On cooperative learning: A conversation with Spencer Kagan. *Educational Leadership*, 47(4): 8-11.

Brookfield, S.D. 1986. *Understanding and facilitating adult learning*. San Francisco: Jossey-Bass Publishers.

Bruffee, K.A. 1984. Collaborative learning and the conversation of mankind. *College English*, 46: 635-652.

Cellar, D.F. and Wade, K. 1988. Effect of behavior modeling on intrinsic motivation and script related recognition. *Journal of Applied Psychology,* 73(2): 181-192.

Cohen, Elizabeth G. 1990. Continuing to cooperate: Prerequisites for persistence. *Phi Delta Kappan,* 72(2): 134-138.

Conger, J.A. and Kanungo, R.N. 1988. The empowerment process: Integrating theory and practice. *Academy of Management Review,* 13: 471-482.

Cross, K. Patricia and Angelo, Thomas A. 1988. *Classroom assessment techniques.* University of Michigan, National Center for Research to Improve Postsecondary Teaching and Learning. Ann Arbor, MI: 30-32.

Damon, W. 1984. Peer education: The untapped potential. *Journal of Applied Developmental Psychology,* 5: 331-343.

DePree, Max. 1989. *Leadership is an art.* New York: Doubleday.

Elman, S.E. and Lynton, E.A. 1985. Assessment in professional education. Columbia, SC: National Conference on Assessment in Higher Education, University of South Carolina.

Fox, W.M. 1987. *Effective group problem-solving.* San Francisco: Jossey-Bass Publishers.

Gioia, Dennis A. and Manz, Charles C. 1985. Linking cognition and behavior: A script processing interpretation of vicarious learning. *Academy of Management Review,* 10(3): 527-539.

Hale, John F. 1986. The boss is away. *Organizational Behavior Teaching Review,* 10(3): 107-111.

Hayes, Elizabeth. 1989. Insights from women's experiences for teaching and learning. In Hayes, E. (Ed.) *Effective teaching styles.* San Francisco: Jossey-Bass Publishers.

Johnson, D.W. and Johnson, R.T. 1987. *Learning together and alone: Cooperative, competitive, and individualistic learning.* Englewood Cliffs, NJ: Prentice-Hall.

Kagan, Spencer. 1990. The structural approach to cooperative learning. *Educational Leadership,* 47(4): 12-15.

Kolb, David. 1984. *Experiential learning.* Englewood Cliffs, NJ: Prentice-Hall.

Kurfiss, J. 1987. The reasoning-centered classroom: Approaches that work. *American Association for Higher Education Bulletin*, March/April: 12-14.

Louis, Meryl R. 1990. The gap in management education. *Selections*, Winter: 1-12.

Lundberg, Craig. 1990. Chronology charting. *Organizational Behavior Teaching Review*, 14(1): 155-156.

Lyons, P. 1991. A social learning paradigm for management education. In *Empowerment in the workplace and classroom*. Proceedings of the Eastern Academy of Management, Hartford, CT: 323-325.

Messick, Samuel. 1988. Testing for success: Implications of new developments in measurement and cognitive science. *Selections*, Autumn: 1-12.

Moore, Carl M. 1987. *Group techniques for idea building*. Beverly Hills, CA: Sage Publications. See Chapter 3, Idea Writing.

Mouton, J.S. and Blake, R.R. 1984. *Synergogy*. San Francisco: Jossey-Bass Publishers.

Pate, L. 1987. Improving managerial decision making. *Journal of Managerial Psychology*, 2(2): 9-15.

Reich, R. 1987. *Tales of a new America*. New York: Times Books.

Serey, Timothy T. 1987. Interviewing the professor: An alternative to the drudgery of the first class. *Organizational Behavior Teaching Review*, 12(2): 111-114.

Sharan, Y. and Sharan, S. 1990. Group investigation expands cooperative learning. *Educational Leadership*, 47(4): 17-21.

Slavin, Robert E. 1983. *Cooperative learning*. New York: Longman.

Taylor, R.R., Worrell, D., and Watson, W. 1986. The behavioral process integration exercise. *Organizational Behavior Teaching Review*, 10: 120-122.

Tubbs, Stewart. 1989. Teacher as leader/developer. *Journal of Professional Studies*, 13(2): 4-16.

Weil, Jeffrey L. 1988. Management experientially taught. *Organizational Behavior Teaching Review*, 12(3): 54-61.

Westmeyer, P. 1988. *Effective teaching in adult and higher education.* Springfield, Ill: Charles C Thomas, Publishers.

Whitcomb, Susanne W. 1981. The action project. *Exchange: The Organizational Behavior Teaching Journal,* 7: 39-41.

Lesson Formats Contents Matrix

PART 1 FORMATS TO ENHANCE PROBLEM-SOLVING AND NEGOTIATION SKILLS

FORMAT	LEARNING FOCUS	MATERIALS NEEDED	SINGLE SESSION	MULTIPLE SESSIONS
The Boss Is Away	Problem-Solving in Teams	YES	YES	YES
Brainstorming the Agenda	Needs Analysis Skills	YES	YES	—
Four Aces Decision-Making Method	Decision-Making Skills	—	YES	—
Policy-Procedures Analysis	Analysis Skills	—	YES	YES
Practitioner's Desk In-Basket	Problem-Solving Skills	YES	YES	—
Problem-Driven Learning	Problem Finding and Solving	—	YES	YES
Reflective Controversy	Research & Collaboration Skills	—	—	YES

PART 2 FORMATS TO ENHANCE PLANNING, ANALYSIS AND COMMUNICATION SKILLS

FORMAT	LEARNING FOCUS	MATERIALS NEEDED	SINGLE SESSION	MULTIPLE SESSIONS
Action Roles–Structured	Communication & Leader Skills	YES	YES	—
Action Roles–Unstructured	Communication & Leader Skills	—	YES	—
Committee Decision	Questioning and Interpretive Skills	—	YES	—
Crossfire Panel	Attitudes Clarification	—	YES	—
Debate with Teams	Research & Planning Skills	—	YES	—
Focused Dialogue	Communication, Interpersonal Skills	—	YES	—
Interviewing the Instructor	Questioning & Interpretive Skills	YES	YES	—
Lecture-Reaction Panel	Attentional, Communication Skills	—	YES	—
Question Sharing	Independent Study & Communication Skills	—	YES	—
Student Expectations	Articulate Needs & Expectations	—	YES	—
Symposium with Critique	Research, Analysis & Communication Skills	—	YES	—

PART 3 FORMATS TO ENHANCE COGNITIVE AND MANAGERIAL SKILLS

FORMAT	LEARNING FOCUS	MATERIALS NEEDED	SINGLE SESSION	MULTIPLE SESSIONS
Background Knowledge Probes	Inventory of Student Knowledge	YES	YES	—
Educating the Consumer	Planning & Study Skills	YES	YES	—
The Forum	Planning & Study Skills	—	YES	—
Idea Exploration	Generate Ideas, Clarification Skills	YES	YES	—
Lecture-Focused Teams	Attentional, Communication Skills	—	YES	—

PART 4 FORMATS TO ENHANCE INTEGRATION AND COOPERATIVE-LEARNING SKILLS

FORMAT	LEARNING FOCUS	MATERIALS NEEDED	SINGLE SESSION	MULTIPLE SESSIONS
The Action Project	Integrate Theory & Practice	YES	—	YES
Chronology Charting	Course Review Skills	YES	YES	—
Clarifying Attitudes Design	Awareness, Evaluation Skills	—	YES	YES
Cooperative Testing	Cognitive Learning	—	—	YES
Group Investigation	Cognitive Learning	—	—	YES
Integration Exercise	Identifying Relationships Skills	YES	YES	YES
Interview by Panel	Research & Collaboration Skills	—	YES	—

FORMAT	LEARNING FOCUS	MATERIALS NEEDED	SINGLE SESSION	MULTIPLE SESSIONS
Jigsaw	Cognitive Learning	—	—	YES
Peer & Individually Mediated Modeling	Create Performance Scripts & Models	YES	—	YES
Performance-Judging Design	Using Evaluation Skills	—	—	YES
The Student-Powered Course	Course Design	YES	YES	YES
Student Teams Achievement Division	Cognitive Learning	YES	—	YES

Index